How to Publish Your Own Book

Secrets from the Inside

Stewart Ferris

summersdale

Summersdale Publishers Ltd
46 West Street
Chichester
West Sussex
PO19 1RP
UK

www.summersdale.com

ISBN: 978-1-84024-519-6

Printed and bound in Great Britain.

Contents

What is self-publishing?

As AN AUTHOR you already know that it isn't easy to persuade a publisher to splash out a considerable chunk of money on editing, designing, printing and marketing your book. It can take years before you strike it lucky, and even if you finally get a contract signed it will be a reminder of who is in charge: the publisher. They will typically hang on to as much as ninety per cent of the income from sales of the book. They have to. They have to pay staff, office bills, print bills, marketing bills and the mortgage on their second home in France. That leaves you, the author, coming to terms with the reality that you won't be able to afford to give up your day job on the royalties from one book alone. Even if you had a dozen published books, assuming they had average sales rather than being bestsellers, you would have to think twice before telling your boss where to stick it and marching confidently home to your new working environment: your shed.

Why not turn the whole thing on its head and put yourself in the position of publisher as well as author? That way you'll keep that ninety per cent as well as your author's ten per cent. Deals don't get much sweeter than that, do they? But, of course, there's a time and a financial investment associated with publishing your own book, and with any investment comes risk. By committing your own cash to the project you have to be prepared for the possibility that you will never see that money again.

It's something that happens to all mainstream publishers too: not every title they produce will sell enough copies to earn back their investment. Publishing is about gambling. Publishers have even been referred to as 'bookies with A-levels'. Experience in the book industry is the only tool available to reduce that risk, and if you're lacking in that department then it's reasonable to say that you'll have a better chance of making a profit by betting two months' wages on a horse than by publishing a book.

Self-publishing means that you, the author, pay for and control all aspects of turning your written words into a format suitable for dissemination amongst the general public. The format could be a printed and bound book or an electronic simulation of a book, known as an eBook, which can be bought and downloaded from the Internet.

Whichever format of book you create, you will be starting a publishing company. Most people do this as sole traders, with no legal formalities to worry about when starting up. Printing isn't difficult, either – you just have to pay a printing firm to do it.

So why do you need this book to help you publish your masterpiece?

What you do between finishing the writing of your book and handing it over to a printer can be the difference between success and failure. Success means a profitable project that actually results in people reading your work; failure means you end up with a pallet of books that sits in your garage gathering dust until you eventually decide to use the unsold copies as firelighters. Worse still, failure means that hardly anyone reads your book.

There's no point in spending your life savings on publishing a book if no one buys it. You want people to enjoy your writing, to think of you as a bona fide author. You want to recoup your investment so that the exercise doesn't appear to your friends as folly.

The self-publishing secrets that can mean the difference between success and failure will be revealed in this book. How do I know those secrets? In 1992 I co-founded Britain's first company to offer all the services an author needs to publish their own book. Over the next decade we ran this self-publishing company alongside our main publishing business, helping hundreds of authors to become publishers and producing books for them in all genres, some of which won awards for self-publishing.

I've watched authors make terrible mistakes in their cover designs which have cost them dearly in terms of lost sales (they would often insist on using their own artwork or photo on the cover, no matter how inappropriate or amateurish). I've seen books poorly edited and full of irrelevant content. But most of all I've seen authors who don't have the faintest idea how to sell their books when they arrive on the lorry from the printers.

I'll tell you all you need to know about the book trade, how to publicise your book (for free), and how to sell it both to shops and to customers directly. You'll also learn the essentials of page layout, cover design, editing and ways to ensure your book does not look self-published – because to a book trade professional, self-published books often stand out a mile and for all the wrong reasons.

This guide will provide you with the equivalent of years of experience in the book industry. The insider tips on the following pages are crucial in reducing the level of risk to which your financial investment will be exposed. I'll start by explaining how to get your book printed and bound. Depending on how much of the process you decide to outsource, some chapters may not appear to be as relevant to you as others, but I'd strongly recommend reading this book as a whole because you can use the information to talk knowledgeably to any freelancers you hire and to demonstrate that you understand what they are doing and that you expect professional results. Since publishing a book is an expensive process, it's necessary also to explain how to recoup that investment by maximising the number of copies sold. Furthermore, we'll be looking at other sources of income from which publishers can benefit: there are many potential revenue streams that ownership of copyright text can generate, and most self-publishers are completely unaware of them.

The final part of this book covers everything you need to know about publishing an eBook. Print and eBook editions are not mutually exclusive: there's nothing wrong with having both editions on sale at the same time.

Reasons why people write books

1. A journey of self-discovery
2. The challenge of completing a whole book
3. A cathartic method of coming to terms with life experiences
4. The desire to tell a good story or impart specialist knowledge
5. The hope that the book will make a profit
6. The satisfaction of knowing that people are reading the book

Of all those reasons, the satisfaction that comes when people read your book is the most powerful motivation of all. It's one thing to know that your friends and family are reading your book, but to find out that a complete stranger has bought it, read it and enjoyed it is a unique thrill that only a published writer can know. Self-publishing can't guarantee that this thrill will happen to you because the process is full of potential pitfalls that can prevent your book achieving a wide exposure, but with this book to guide you safely through them you'll have the best possible chance of success.

What's the difference between vanity publishing and self-publishing?

BEFORE WE GO any further it's important to understand exactly what *vanity publishing* is and how it differs from self-publishing. Vanity publishing, sometimes known as *subsidy* publishing or *partnership* publishing, can work something like this:

1. An author sees an advert in a Sunday paper that reads something along the lines of 'Authors wanted – all genres considered'. (You should know that real publishers don't pay to advertise for authors to submit manuscripts. Even small publishers receive plenty more submissions than they could ever hope to publish.)

2. This rather optimistic author, who has just finished writing a book, submits it to the address in the advert.

3. The author receives a glowing letter of praise for the book together with an offer to publish. (This letter of praise is often completely generic because no one at the publishing company has actually read the book.)

4. A contract arrives, promising high royalty rates for sales, and the author gets excited because their dream seems to be coming true.

5. The author spots a small snag in the contract: instead of the publisher paying the author an advance on royalties, this publisher is requesting that the author 'shares the cost' of publishing the book by paying a sum of money to them. It is worded carefully to make it sound like a joint venture with at least half of the risk being taken on by the publisher, but what the author doesn't realise is that the amount of money they are being asked to hand over is enough to pay for the entire production costs of the book plus the publisher's profit margin. Nevertheless, the author is blinded by the flattering comments about the book and by the prospect of seeing it in print, and therefore reaches for their credit card before noticing the next slight problem in the contract…

6. The publisher only prints a handful of copies of the book. After these initial copies have been sold, books will be printed to order, one at a time.

There's nothing wrong with vanity publishing if you want to see your book printed in the nicest, simplest way. Just hand over the cash and wait for it to arrive. But remember that the vanity publisher has no interest in selling your book. They have already made their profit from you and don't need to go to the effort of actually visiting bookshops and sending out press releases. Your book will be available for any high street or Internet bookshops to buy, but this simply means it's on a database with every other book in print so that if a customer asks for it the shop can order it. Vanity publishing is an expensive, luxury service which gives you almost zero chance of earning back your investment. You don't even own outright the books that you've paid to have printed.

Compare this to self-publishing, and you'll see why the two should not be confused. A self-publishing author can still employ the services of experts who will arrange the cover design, typesetting and printing of the books, just as a publisher would, but at the end of the process you will own all of the stock that you paid to have printed. Not only that, you'll have more books for your money. Hundreds or even thousands more. All the money earned from sales is yours to keep and the responsibility for selling them lies in your hands, as does the motivation.

The term 'vanity publishing' applies to companies that specialise in producing books using only money supplied by their authors. However, occasionally a mainstream publisher will strike a deal with an author that requires them to pay a subsidy. This might happen because the book fits the publisher's list but its market is too narrow to be likely to generate a profit, or the publisher's print budgets are fully allocated and the only option open to them is to share costs with the author. Sometimes the author has access to more customers than the publisher could reach and therefore it makes sense for the author to be the primary investor in the project. In these circumstances the cost-sharing author is more likely to make a return on the investment because the publisher has a sales and marketing infrastructure.

Why should I self-publish?

GETTING A BOOK accepted by a mainstream publishing company is a slow and often frustrating process. It's not just the fact that a string of rejections is hurtful – the weeks and months between each negative decision can test your patience and drain your enthusiasm for the book you've worked so hard to write.

Self-publishing is about taking control over what happens to your book. You remove the need for someone else to fall in love with your writing. Besides, even if an editor in a publishing house were to read your book and think it was exquisitely written, the decision to sign you up would also depend on factors beyond your control such as the success of similar books on the market, the cash flow and budget of the company, and the decisions of senior management who can, on a whim, decide to cease publishing books like yours.

In addition to reducing the time between finishing the final edit of your book and seeing it on sale in a bookshop, self-publishing means that you can potentially make more substantial profits than an author on a royalty. Why accept ten or fifteen per cent of the income from sales when you could have one hundred per cent? I made the decision to self-publish my first book when I realised that I might make more money than I'd receive on a meagre royalty.

Of course this is meaningless if you don't make enough from sales to cover the costs of typesetting and printing. If the book doesn't sell well, an author on a royalty will do better than a self-published author. This is because the author on a royalty will usually receive an advance which is non-returnable in the event that the book fails to sell, whereas the self-published author will have paid out a significant amount of cash. But if a book is successful, and success is usually measured in terms of at least one or two thousand copies sold, the self-published author stands to make more money.

There is an argument that a self-published book is less likely to be successful. Self-publishers are newcomers to the book business and it's harder for them to achieve good sales figures than it is for established firms. Therefore even though a published author earns less per book than does a self-published author it's likely that the former will benefit from a higher volume of sales. But this doesn't have to be the case. Self-publishers can actually out-sell their competitors. You can too if you follow the advice in this book. With greater unit sales and all the net income yours to keep, it can make sound financial sense to self-publish.

How can I choose the right title and subtitle for my book?

MANY BOOKS THAT you see in bookshops do not display the original title thought up by the author. Publishers commonly have to think of a better title in order to increase the selling potential of the book. The title and subtitle combination that you choose for your book can mean the difference between success and failure. Those few words printed on the front cover have the power to grab your attention and your wallet. The title tells a potential reader what the book is about, and the subtitle gives them a reason to buy it. 'How to Publish Your Own Book' is the title of this book, but the line 'Secrets from the Inside' gently nudges the reader towards a purchasing decision, which will be backed up by the blurb on the back cover.

It's not just the readers who need to be attracted by your title: bookshop managers are more likely to stock a book that has a clever, distinctive, topical or simply appropriate title. To this end, spend some time studying the titles and subtitles of competing books to see if they use wordplay, idioms, clichés with a twist or a particular vocabulary. Try to match the 'feel' that these books evoke when choosing your own title.

Novels don't usually need a subtitle, but there's something very similar to it, known as a 'tag line', which is worth considering. Often the tag line will only form part of the marketing literature for a novel and won't appear on the cover, but printing it above the title didn't do any harm to Kate Mosse's hit novel, *Labyrinth*. It has a one-word title, but the cover bears the enticing tag line, 'Three secrets. Two women. One grail.'

What does the process of publishing actually involve?

PUBLISHING COMPANIES CREATE books on a virtual production line. All the work they do is referred to as 'pre-press' because it's everything that happens before the manuscript reaches the printing presses. Remember that publishers are not printers. You won't find a printing press in any book publisher's office: they always outsource the printing to specialist firms.

While some of these stages are underway, publishers will be carrying out tasks not directly connected with the preparation of printing files. They will be trying to sell the book and to publicise it. This isn't something that a self-publisher can easily do whilst immersed in the detail of editing and designing their book, but don't wait for the finished book to arrive before giving sales and publicity any attention. The moment your PDF is with the printer you should start trying to generate demand for your book. Ideally, make a start on the sales and publicity side several months ahead of the publication date. Techniques for advance marketing will be covered later in this book.

WHAT DOES THE PROCESS OF PUBLISHING ACTUALLY INVOLVE?

The pre-press process involves a number of steps, not all of which are applicable to every book project:

1.   Structuring the manuscript

2.   Editing the manuscript

3.   Scanning and altering drawings, photographs or diagrams

4.   Typesetting the manuscript

5.   Adding footnotes and captions

6.   Creating the contents page, index and copyright page

7.   Proofreading the typeset pages for errors

8.   Designing the front cover, spine and back cover (and inside flaps if a jacketed hardback)

9.   Obtaining an ISBN and a bar code

10. Setting the selling price

11. Creating a PDF of the insides and the cover

The first two stages listed above are covered in detail in the sections on redrafting in another book in this series, *How to be a Writer*. These stages are important for any writer, but as a self-publisher editing and proofreading are your responsibility, so the guidelines given here tackle the subject purely from that perspective.

Structuring the manuscript

WHEN THE FIRST draft of your book has been written you should begin a long process of improvements before committing the words to printed form. The first thing to do is to look at the overall structure of the book. Would it work better if the first two chapters were swapped around? Do the chapters progress in a logical manner? Does it need a subplot? Should there be a progressive character arc? Does it need more comedy or more gravitas? Structuring your book doesn't mean changing the odd word – it's about looking objectively at the order of the chapters and the progression of the story or the argument and deciding whether it should be altered. A book can benefit from restructuring if it means that the new opening chapter is stronger, if the chapter endings become cliffhangers to tempt people to keep reading, or if the pace and balance of the book are improved.

Editing the manuscript

WHEN THE OVERALL structure of the book is in place you can start the lengthy process of fine-tuning the text. Self-discipline needs to be applied at this stage to counter the temptation to print the book before it's ready. When trying to get published at the expense of a mainstream publisher, the pressure is on to make the manuscript as perfect as you can in order to increase your chances of acceptance. With self-publishing it's not a question of acceptance, but it's important to strive for the standards you would have set yourself for submission to another publisher.

In fact, that publishing company would have then set an editor or a team of editors to work on the manuscript to make it even better still. So as a self-publisher you have to aim to *exceed* the standard of editing that you would be able to achieve on your own. That's why you should take advantage of friends to look for errors that you may have missed. The promise of an acknowledgement in the book and a free copy is usually sufficient reward. It doesn't matter if they're especially well-read or not: if your friends are all English teachers it's probably an advantage, but anyone should be able to notice if you've typed a word twice or missed a word out.

Not everyone notices the same things, so I recommend printing at least five copies of your manuscript for five sets of eyes to peruse. When the pages come back you can assimilate all of the valid corrections into your master copy.

Mistakes in your text will be pointed out to you that are completely obvious, staring at you from the page. And yet you didn't spot them, despite several redrafting efforts and your own proofreading. The problem for authors is that when typing a line of their book their brains sometimes move ahead to the next line before their fingers have finished tapping out the letters. The resulting typed sentence becomes contracted, missing out a word or a letter. When the author later reads the line back it seems perfect. The mistake is invisible. This is because the author knows the correct sequence of words and is reciting them rather than reading them. It takes another person to spot this kind of common error. Failing that, the author needs to spend a few weeks or months away from the book in order to come back to it with objective eyes. If the word sequence is forgotten by then, the mistake should be plainly visible.

Hiring a freelance proofreader is a sensible option if your budget allows for it. The more friends you can rope in to check your text for you the better, but a qualified proofreader should be able to pick up everything they find and more. The Society for Editors and Proofreaders has a website that lists over four hundred members and their qualifications and contact details: www.sfep.org.uk. The site will also give an indication of the likely cost of hiring someone to proof your book.

A belt and braces approach is to use friends *and* to hire a freelance proofreader. The more feedback you get, the fewer mistakes will slip through the net.

Copyright protection for your manuscript

At this stage, when you have a completed and edited manuscript, you might want to take steps to prove your copyright to the work. You don't need to do anything to copyright your writing: anything you write is automatically your copyright. The only thing that matters is being able to prove that you wrote it in case someone steals your writing and tries to pass it off as their own. Such cases are rare, but you can easily prepare for them by employing any of the following methods:

1. Mail a copy of your manuscript to yourself. Check that the postmark is legible when it arrives, and, if so, don't open it. File it away so that it can be opened by a judge if it ever came to court. This method does not offer total protection, because a postmark can be faked.

2. Keep every draft and all of your notes and research that contributed to the final book. This demonstrates the progress you made

towards the end product. Anyone who simply copies your text will not have any different versions to prove they wrote it. Keep papers and computer files.

3. Register your manuscript with a company such as The UK Copyright Service. They can record the date it was received by them and verify you as the author. This is more suited to unpublished works, because if you wait until the book is published before registering it with them then your printed edition serves the same purpose. Their website is: www.copyrightservice.co.uk.

4. If your book is co-written with someone else, create and sign an agreement that clearly states how you intend the copyright in the work to be shared. Usually this would mean an equal share of the copyright between the authors, but you may wish to split the share unequally to reflect different levels of input. Also, by making an agreement now, you can avoid arguments that occur if the book becomes a bestseller and people start to get greedy.

Scanning and altering drawings, photographs or diagrams

ANY ILLUSTRATIVE MATERIAL for the insides or the cover of your book will have to be scanned (unless it is already in a digital format, such as a photograph taken on a digital camera and copied into your computer as an image file) so that it can be inserted into the typesetting software for laying out alongside the text. Even the cheapest consumer scanner these days is capable of scanning at a higher quality than the expensive machines professional publishers were using just a decade ago. You might have an 'all-in-one' printer which has a scanner on the top, or a stand-alone scanner. It's possible to get good enough results with either kind, but only if you understand the basic rules of scanning and preparing images for print. These rules vary according to the type of image being scanned, but in general all images should be scanned at their natural size (or smaller if larger than the intended page size for your book). If you set your scanner to enlarge a small image, such as a slide, the resolution must be enhanced accordingly.

You should also avoid compressing the image size too much. Compression technologies were developed to reduce the file size of images. When hard disk space was expensive it was essential for still images to be compressed to save space inside the computer. Small file sizes also meant that the images could be processed more quickly in documents. File size is no longer a problem for modern computers (although it's a huge problem for the Internet, but that's another story), so avoid compressing files where possible. When saving as a JPEG, select the maximum image quality, minimum compression end of the slider. The higher the compression, the lower the quality.

Black and white line drawings

If your illustrations are simple black on white, with no shades of grey, then they should be scanned at 600 dpi in bitmap mode. This works best with illustrations made using only a black pen, or when scanning printed text, and the reproduction quality is very high even on relatively rough printed papers, such as are often used in novels. They should be saved as TIFF images, ready to be imported into the typesetting software.

Black and white photos and shaded images

These should be scanned at 300 dpi in greyscale ('grayscale' according to American software) mode. The files should be saved in JPEG format with the minimum level of compression used.

Colour photos and images

These should be scanned at 300 dpi in RGB colour mode, but they will need to be converted to CMYK colour mode before saving as JPEG files with minimum compression. Most home scanners are unable to scan directly into CMYK mode, so the image file needs to be converted from RGB in a photo-editing programme such as Photoshop. The reason for the conversion to CMYK is that colours can be created either using a mixture of three colours – red, green and blue (RGB); or using a mixture of four colours – cyan, magenta, yellow and black (CMYK). Computer screens are better at displaying images in RGB mode. Because the colour information is made up from just three component parts the file size is correspondingly smaller too. Printing presses use CMYK to print colour images, though. Four pots of ink are combined to create high quality colour photographs and illustrations. So the PDF you supply to the printer should contain colour images made from CMYK combinations rather than RGB.

What is resolution?

The scanning of an image turns it into rows of tiny dots. In simple terms, imagine a chess board with some of the white squares painted black:

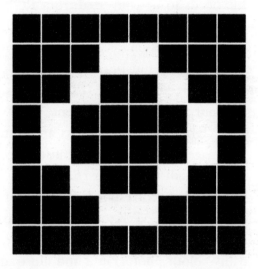

A very crude circle has been created by turning 'on' or 'off' simple blocks on a grid of sixty-four squares. It doesn't look very pretty, but it's essentially how a computer 'sees' an image when it has been scanned. The only difference is that the computer uses a grid of more than eight by eight: the standard number of blocks in just one square inch is three hundred. Each square then becomes so small that it looks like a dot, and the awkward angles shown above start to look smoother when the squares are reduced: ▓. The number of dots (or pixels) per inch is referred to as 'dpi'.

Televisions and computer screens also display images in this way. High definition televisions have a grid of about a thousand dots across the entire screen and eight hundred dots down. Each of these dots can be displayed in thousands of different colours. All of the dots on the screen are changed twenty-four times every second, which is fast enough to create the illusion of movement and real life. But actually all you are seeing is a rapid sequence of scanned dots based on the same principle in the above grid.

Transparencies, negatives and slides

Slides need to be enlarged from their original size. If you scan at 300 dpi and quadruple the image size, the resolution is effectively reduced to just 75 dpi. Slides should therefore be scanned according to this simple formula: whatever the factor by which you want to enlarge the original slide size should be multiplied by 300 dpi. So to scan a 15 mm-wide slide suitable for enlargement to a width of 150 mm (about A5 size) requires a scanning resolution of 3,000 dpi. A scanner can't scan a slide unless it has a transparency adapter fitted. This is like a second, mini-scanner mounted in the lid in order to provide light on both sides of the slide. Without it your scan will be a black mess. Negatives scan well with a transparency adapter, but Photoshop will need to invert the image to create a positive. Once the image is scanned it should be adjusted to 300 dpi at its new size, converted to CMYK if a colour image and saved as a JPEG.

It's important to spend time improving every image that you intend to include in your book. If a scan is crooked, rotate it in Photoshop until it's straight. If it has dirt marks on it, carefully zoom in and clean them up. Colours, brightness, contrast and sharpness can also be enhanced in Photoshop. It's a powerful piece of software that takes time and quite a substantial manual to understand. If you intend publishing illustrated books on a regular basis after your first self-publishing venture is completed, then it's worth taking the trouble to invest in and master this software. If your book is likely to be a one-off, then it makes more sense to attempt the image manipulation needed using cheaper software, or free software, such as can be found bundled with digital cameras, downloaded from the Internet or given away free on a computer magazine covermount.

Some free image manipulation software to try

Paint.NET
http://www.getpaint.net

SoftDeposit.com has links to a number of different free, shareware and limited period trial software packages for image manipulation.
http://www.softdeposit.com/index-71-1.html.

Typesetting the manuscript

THE MOST NOTICEABLE leap forward in the whole self-publishing process is getting your book typeset. This transforms it from a word processor document into something that resembles the finished pages of a book. It's an exciting moment for an author when they see their book typeset for the first time.

Typesetting is definitely something that you can do yourself, but there are many traps a novice can fall into so it's best to get some training first. I hired a freelance typesetter for my first two self-published books. During the typesetting of the second one I watched him at work and realised that it didn't look too complicated. In fact, eighty per cent of the job is done automatically by the software. It's the way in which you design the final twenty per cent of the book that can mean the difference between something that looks professional and something that looks little better than a raw manuscript.

It's beyond the realms of this little book to give detailed instructions for all the main typesetting software packages, but I'll explain the process in general terms to give you an understanding of what you might be letting yourself in for if you decide to try this yourself, and what to look out for if you pay someone else to do it. The principles explained here, when used in conjunction with the software manual, should help you get professional results faster. Remember also to look at the layout styles of books similar to the one you wish to publish, and try to emulate their best aspects.

So what is it that the software (this was PageMaker – since replaced by InDesign) was doing to typeset the book automatically? It basically flowed all of the text into the framework of the page margins throughout the book, like water filling a bottle, and with a single click it turned all of that text into the style of font that would be used for the main body of text. The whole thing had taken just a couple of minutes, and there before me were pages that looked as if they had leapt right out of a book.

To prepare for this automatic typesetting phase requires a little bit of set-up, which for an experienced typesetter will only take a short while. The first thing to do is to create a new document and tell the software what page size you want and how big the margins should be. Then you define the different styles of text that you think you'll be needing. The majority of your book will usually consist of 'body text': choose a font for it, choose a size and a paragraph style (usually justified with a small indent for the first line). Then create a much larger version of that style, change the paragraph alignment to centred and call it something like 'chapter heading'. Step the size down a few points and call it 'sub chapter'. Those are your basic ingredients. Now import your text, flow it into the document, 'select all' and click on 'body text'. Now the entire book is set in body text, but the job is far from finished.

The next stage is to 'tag' all of the different text elements. Click on the chapter headings and choose your predefined 'chapter heading' style from the style list. Do the same for sub chapters. If there are captions, define a font style and tag those. Create a version of body text for the first paragraph of each chapter which is identical to body text in every respect except that it has no indent for the first line. I usually call this style 'flush' because it's flush with the left-hand margin. Create as many styles as you need and tag every paragraph of text appropriately. Note that because you began by tagging the entire book as body text, most of the paragraphs don't need to be touched. Just tag anything that is not body text.

When tagging the text, don't worry about positioning it correctly. Chapter headings will be all over the place, sometimes at the bottom of the page, and the whole thing will look messy. That's fine, it's part of the first sweep that you make through the book.

Defining styles in this way makes the whole job much easier because if you later decide that you want your chapter headings to be in a different font or left-aligned instead of centred, all you have to do is edit your chapter style definition and the chapter headings throughout the book will automatically update themselves. All you then need to do is to check the book to make sure your changes haven't thrown anything out of alignment.

Typesetting involves several sweeps through the book. Having tagged everything, the next sweep involves aligning the beginnings of each chapter in order to gauge the number of pages the book is running to. Page extent is something you should decide on before you begin typesetting if you're planning a full print run, rather than print on demand. The manufacturing process used in print on demand involves single sheets of paper and allows complete flexibility in page count. It only has to be divisible by two. For full print runs large sheets of paper are used on the printing press, each one containing thirty-two pages. These sheets are folded and then trimmed to create a thirty-two page section. If you look inside any mass-market book from your shelf you'll find the pages are divisible by thirty-two. This book has 160 pages, so it consists of five complete sections of thirty-two. If I wanted to print a book with just 150 pages, the giant sheets of paper would still be the same size, and would simply contain ten blank pages. I'd still be paying the same price as for 160 pages. As the extent of the book increases by every thirty-two pages, there is a corresponding increase in the printing costs. For that reason you may want to limit yourself to a particular page count.

If you need your book to fit to a multiple of thirty-two pages then now is the time to get the page count correct. Let's assume you're aiming for 160 pages, and that having tagged everything and approx-imately laid out the positions of the chapter beginnings you're looking at 200 pages. You really don't want to pay the extra for another section of thirty-two pages, which means that bringing the page count down by eight pages isn't enough: you need to reduce it by forty pages.

No problem. Happens all the time.

There are various typesetting tricks of the trade that will enable you to reduce the length of the book:

1. Adjust the margins. Typesetting software will automatically adjust the entire book if you alter the margin width. Just one millimetre taken from each of the four margins could remove several pages from the book's length.

2. Reduce the size of the body text. A subtle reduction, such as half a point, can again cut several pages from the book.

3. Reduce the leading. Leading is the gap between the lines of text. The default settings provided by typesetting software will usually look perfectly all right, but tighten them up a little in the style definition and some more pages will disappear from the end.

4. Tighten the tracking. Tracking is the gap between the letters in the text. The default setting is a medium tracking, but setting it to 'tight' or 'very tight' can shave a few pages from the count.

5. Look at the opening pages – do you really need to have a dedication on its own page? Could it share a page with the acknowledgements? Could your 'About the Author' text fit at the

bottom of the copyright page? Do you have a half-title page followed by a blank page and then a full title page (a common style that is more often used when padding is needed to add the pages)? If so then replacing them with a single full title page will save valuable space.

6. Do you have any chapters that end with a small number of lines on a page? If so, with a little tweaking, it will be possible to 'suck' those lines back onto the previous page and therefore save an entire page (assuming you've set the book with each chapter starting on a new page). The methods used to tweak the text include: tightening the tracking on paragraphs that end with a single word on the last line to suck that word up onto the previous line; pulling the text down over the bottom margin by one line (make sure the page numbers are set sufficiently low to allow for this); reducing the leading on some pages to allow an extra line on the page; widening the text area over the side margins by a millimetre or two in order to suck up an extra line on that page.

7. Let your chapters start wherever they fall, rather than putting them on a new page. This isn't appropriate for all books, but it's very common in fiction. Some typesetters like to start each chapter on a right-facing page. This is a huge extravagance if space is limited, as it often results in the page facing the new chapter being left completely blank.

8. Reduce the size of the chapter headings and the gap between the chapter heading and the first paragraph.

All of these book-shortening techniques will, of course, work in reverse if you want your page count to be higher.

The techniques will all completely upset the approximate layout that you have achieved up to this point, but that's fine – it's part of the process. The next step is to sweep through the book again, lining up the chapter beginnings as you did before. Now check the length and make further tweaks if necessary until you are within a handful of pages of your target amount. That's a handful fewer rather than too many, of course. When fine-tuning the book's layout the length may alter in the process and it's best to have three or four pages to spare in order to absorb any subsequent expansion.

There are simple tricks to improve the elegance of a book's layout. This book uses a style that involves capitalising the first three words of the body text in each chapter using 'small caps'. The first letter is a full-size capital, and the others are reduced-size capitals. Another elegant method is to use drop caps. This is when the first letter of the first paragraph of each chapter is two or three lines in height, and the rest of the text wraps neatly around it. Typesetting software can create drop caps very easily (but don't try to edit the text of a paragraph with a drop cap without removing the drop cap first – otherwise you'll end up with a horrible mess).

If you decide to try typesetting your book yourself, make sure you build in enough time to practise using the software. It takes time to typeset a book if you haven't done so before. I typeset this book myself, and it took me nearly two days. I can typeset books with simpler layouts than this one (with none of these awkward boxes and inserts everywhere) in as little as a couple of hours. Novels are particularly straightforward. Heavily illustrated books would take me up to a week to typeset. A book with a magazine-style layout, where images and text flow around each other in complex ways and the layout on every page is different, would take many weeks to complete. These speeds reflect the fact that I've typeset hundreds of books: a newcomer will always take two or three times as long to do the same job.

The great thing about typesetting is that the result you want to achieve can usually be reached in three different ways. One of them will take many hours, working laboriously. One will take a few minutes. The other might take just a few seconds.

Take the creation of a contents page, for instance. You can type out the chapter titles in a list, then look up the page numbers one at a time and enter them onto the contents page, then line everything up using the space bar or the tab button. That's the slowest way. Or you could copy and paste the chapter titles one at a time onto the contents page, print it out, and write the page numbers on the printout as you go through the book on the screen, then type them onto the contents page and align everything using multiple full stops between the chapter title and the page number to which you then apply the 'force justify' command to make it line up smartly. That's a little quicker, but still a very involved process. Or you could tick the 'include in table of contents' box in your predefined chapter heading style, click 'generate table of contents' and paste it on the appropriate page. All you need then do is adjust the font and typeset according to preference.

A brief history of typesetting

The word 'typesetting' originally referred to the old printing practice of physically lining up blocks of metal type and setting them in a frame which would be inked and then stamped against the paper. Typesetting in this manner was a highly skilled profession, but desktop publishing caused a revolution in this industry. Out went the factory jobs, replaced by a small number of office workers sitting at their computers.

The Apple Macintosh computer in the mid-1980s was the first successful microcomputer to offer 'what you see is what you get' design capability. Other computers had allowed pages to be laid out in book format, but it was done by typing in complex codes around the text, telling the computer the width of the margin and where to put the page number, etc. What the Apple did was to allow designers to see their page on the screen exactly as it would look on the final page. It didn't matter that the screen was smaller than a letter box: the future of publishing had arrived.

Software such as PageMaker and Quark Express quickly dominated the industry. They were created to enable publishers to design all the elements of their pages on-screen, including images. These pages were then printed via a laser printer to create camera-ready copy, or CRC. The CRC was then handed to the printing company to be photographed using a giant camera to create film from which the printing presses could print the pages. In the late 1990s the CRC-to-film stage of the process was bypassed thanks to the development of PostScript files and then PDFs. Now, thanks to e-mail and PDFs, it's possible to typeset a book and e-mail it directly to the printer.

The details of typesetting won't be your concern if you choose to outsource your typesetting to a freelancer, a printer or a self-publishing company. All you need concern yourself with is whether the pages look professional, stylish and interesting. Before they start show them examples of typesetting layouts that you admire. It's like showing a magazine photo of a celebrity to your hairdresser and asking for a cut in the same style. It simplifies the job for them and reduces the chances that you'll be unhappy with the result. The typesetter may try to get away with doing the least amount of work possible, so you should make it clear to them what you expect. If you want a layout which is livened up by boxes of text, images, decorative borders and text effects such as drop caps, you should explain that in the brief before work begins.

Always start each typesetting sweep at the beginning – never work backwards. When you make a change to the layout, such as enlarging the gap between the chapter title and the first paragraph, it never affects the preceding pages but it always affects all of the following pages.

What are 'giveaway' signs of amateur typesetting?

WHETHER YOU TYPESET the book yourself or you hire a professional, check the results carefully for the following signs of amateurism.

Double quotation marks

We are taught at school to put speech in double quotation marks, and amateur publishers set their books using this style. Whether you're setting the pages yourself or paying a typesetter to do the job for you, make sure you perform an automatic search and replace in your word processor file to change each double quotation mark to a single one before the text is imported into the typesetting software. The only time it is acceptable to have double quotation marks in a book is when your speaking character quotes someone else's words. For example:

'You'll never guess what she told me,' said John. 'She said "I'm pregnant".'

Huge paragraph indents

Set your paragraph indents to no more than 4 mm. Anything more will start to look like a self-published book.

No paragraph indents and a gap between every paragraph

Books can be typeset without paragraph indents, but you would only do it that way if there was a gap between each paragraph instead. Books with gaps between every paragraph tend to be relatively short with regard to the number of words, and relatively light with regards to the tone of the content. It's a useful technique for increasing the page count of a short text, but it wouldn't look good to use this layout style for something substantial like a novel.

Ragged text

Ragged text, or left-aligned text, can be a legitimate stylistic decision, but unless you really know what you're doing it would be far safer to stick to justified text (laid out to a straight vertical line on the right hand side of the text).

Too much hyphenation

Having line after line ending with words that are split over two lines using hyphens can look ugly. My preference is to turn off hyphenation when typesetting a book, and only to turn it on for individual paragraphs where it is the only means of avoiding the big gaps that can sometimes occur between words when justification is used.

Huge gaps between words in justified text

Having just recommended justified text it's important to be aware of a common problem that occurs when long words appear close together in justified text: big gaps. Computers create justified text by altering the gaps between words. When a line contains ten words it can be justified by dividing any alterations in the gaps between nine of them, so the spacing is unlikely to look odd. But if you have only four words on the line then the computer has only three gaps to stretch in order to align the line. This can result in ugly, big gaps. The phenomenon is worse the narrower the page column width, and is particularly noticeable when website addresses form part of the text.

Paragraph indents at the start of chapters and after a gap or picture

Typesetting convention is to have the first paragraph of a chapter aligned flush with the left-hand margin on the first line. It's also more professional looking not to indent after a gap in the text or after a picture.

Bad photos

Don't scan your photos and insert them in your book without considering their quality and relevance to the text. Think about cropping the edges, or perhaps cutting out the background entirely. Adjust them: if they are scans of printed photos they will need to be lightened. Make sure the dpi settings and the file format are correct.

Text too close to the spine or the outer page edges

Think about your margins when typesetting. Equal margins either side of the block of text may look good on the computer screen, but what happens when that page is printed and bound into a book? Part of the margin on one side will be eaten up by the binding of the book. If it is tightly bound and difficult to open it might mean that some of the text alongside that margin is impossible to view. Therefore you should always allow a few extra millimetres for the margins that form the spine of the book. The top and bottom margins should be spacious enough for your running headers and page numbers. The outer margin, plus the top and bottom margins, all need to allow for any inaccuracy in the printer's trimming equipment. The pages may be cut up to 3 mm too big or too small. There's nothing you can do about that as it's part of the small print in the contract to print a book, so you just have to make allowances for it in the design. As an example, the margin settings for this book are: 23 mm for the inside margin, 19 mm for the outside margin, 20 mm for the top and 20 mm for the bottom.

Widows and orphans

A widow is a single line of text at the top of a page that is the final line of a paragraph on the previous page. If it is a complete line then it doesn't look too bad, but if it's just one or two words at the top of the page followed by a new paragraph then it looks horrible.

An orphan is the first line of a paragraph that begins at the bottom of one page and continues on to the next.

These are classic typesetting errors that can be seen in the output of most self-publishers, but are easily avoided by paying attention to the top and bottom of each page when typesetting and adjusting where necessary.

Adding footnotes and captions

FOOTNOTES ARE ADDED to a book at the typesetting stage. They make the job of typesetting much more complex and slow, and this will be reflected in the price if you're paying someone to do it. You should ensure that any footnotes or captions that need to be added to the book are supplied to the typesetter in a Word document from which they can copy and paste the text. Never allow them to type anything themselves unless you're standing over their shoulders watching closely.

Creating the contents page, index and copyright page

THE INDEX AND CONTENTS page cannot be created until the book has been typeset, allowing sufficient space for inserting those items. Typesetting software can create a table of contents automatically, as outlined previously. Indexing works in a similar way, but it's a slower process. Each word you want to index needs to be flagged in the typesetting software so that it knows to include it. Only once all of the relevant words in the entire book have been flagged appropriately can the index be automatically generated.

As for the copyright page, take a look at page two of this book. It's a page that most readers never bother even to glance at. The information contained there is primarily for the benefit of the publisher and the bookseller, but it also contains information for people wanting to contact the publisher or to find out who owns the copyright to the book.

Publishers' copyright pages vary slightly in their layout and content, and some will appear at the back of the book instead of at the front, but there are certain key elements that they all contain.

1. The copyright statement. This is normally the author's name, followed by the copyright symbol '©' and the year of publication. Sometimes the publisher is listed as owning the copyright instead of the author. Since in your case they are one and the same it is up to you to choose. To obtain the © symbol in Microsoft Word click 'Insert' and 'Symbol' and select the symbol from the grid.

2. The rights statement 'All rights reserved'. This means that you reserve all of the copyrights and sub-rights associated with your book, such as film rights and translation rights, and that no one can exploit any of those rights without your permission.

3. Assertion of moral rights. Any versions, adaptations, legally licensed sub-right editions (such as the film of the book) must credit you as the author if this statement is printed in your book. It seems a little heavy-handed for a first-time, self-published book, but it doesn't do any harm to include it and thereby protect your rights for the future. Just insert your name into the phrase: 'The right of [YOUR NAME] to be identified as the author of this work has been asserted in accordance with sections 77 and 78 of the Copyright, Designs and Patents Act 1988.'

4. Condition of Sale. This prohibits the subsequent resale of this book in a new cover design.

5. The address of the publisher. This is essential for a variety of reasons. If someone wanted to purchase rights to adapt the book as a stage play, or to publish a translated edition, or to pay you for any of the sub-rights from which you could benefit, they will need to know where to contact you. Shops may also need to know where you are both to order new copies and to return unsold stock. If you feel

uncomfortable about printing your home address in your book, or if you are thinking of moving house, you can hire a PO Box address. Many of my early books were printed with a PO Box address in them. The Post Office will deliver PO Box-addressed mail to your home for an additional fee.

6. The website of the publisher. Even if your web presence is just a single page depicting your book cover and its blurb, it's important to have a website.

7. The ISBN. As a new publisher you will be issued a thirteen-digit ISBN, so there's no need to list a ten-digit one as well. This book has both because Summersdale is currently still using up its allocation of ten-digit numbers. Eventually all books will carry only thirteen-digit ISBNs.

8. The print statement. If you know the printer who will manufacture your book you can list their name and address. If not, you can simply name the country in which you expect to print it.

Proofreading the typeset pages for errors

THE TYPESETTING PROCESS is one in which errors can easily be introduced into your pristine text. Sometimes the typesetter needs to cut and paste text to make things fit the desired layout and it's possible for the paste to be forgotten following a cut if a distraction occurs at that point, such as a phone call. It sometimes happens that the cursor is left in the text and an accidental keystroke adds or removes a letter from a word. It could be that whole pages have been accidentally lost. If the typesetter is required to type in corrections or captions you can virtually guarantee that mistakes will be made. However diligent the typesetter, they will never be as careful with your text as you yourself would be. That's why it's essential to build enough time into your publishing schedule to check the typeset pages twice: firstly to look at the layout to make sure the styles are consistent and to your liking; secondly to read the entire book to make sure no clangers have crept in.

Designing the front cover, spine and back cover (and inside flaps if a jacketed hardback)

IN TERMS OF selling your book and having the best chance of earning back the money you put into it, the front cover design is the single most important part of the whole publishing process. You may be an excellent writer but no one knows that until they buy the book to read it. They can't see whether you're blessed with literary talents or not when they first see the book in a bookshop. But they can see the cover design, and it is this aspect of the book that will persuade them to give your writing a chance. As with typesetting, cover design is something you can do yourself. However, the level of design skills required is much higher. You need a combination of technical and artistic skills to create a professional-looking cover for your book. If you've never designed something before then frankly you'd be mad not to outsource this.

Designers need to be briefed as to what you need. The brief will include:

1. The title
2. The subtitle (if any)
3. Your name (or *nom de plume*)
4. Any other text you'd like to see on the cover
5. The size of the book
6. The genre within which the book fits
7. A summary of the themes and ideas in the book
8. Any images you may have which might be suitable to incorporate into the design
9. Any restrictions, such as limiting the cover design to two colours
10. Any extravagances you'd like, such as embossing or foiling
11. Examples of current and recent bestselling books from the same genre

A good designer will offer more than one interpretation of the brief. Taste is a personal thing and you might not like everything they come up with, but if they present you with three different options there's a reasonable chance that you might like one of them. But if none of them appeals, what can you do? The worst thing you can do is to accept a cover design that you know to be weak just because you don't want to reject all of someone's work or to incur additional design costs. It may cost more at this stage to hire another designer to have a go, but if it results in a more appealing cover you'll earn that money back in the long run.

Make sure the designer knows the conventions of the genre and follows them. It's no good making a novel look like a cookery book or a children's book look like a university textbook. Books sell more copies when their design fits an established genre because customers are more comfortable with them; they feel they can trust the author to deliver because the author's book seems to match other books they've read. A great example of this is the cover design of *The Da Vinci Code*, which spawned dozens of imitations. If you want to publish a thriller, it certainly wouldn't hurt to copy the typeface, colours, image style and text positioning of Dan Brown's bestseller. Many publishers have done so and have benefited from it. Some of the biggest-selling titles I've ever published have been ones that were designed to look like 'sister titles' to established bestsellers in the same genre.

Like most things, book design follows fashion. It's no good taking inspiration from the cover of a book published a decade ago. Bookshops like to arrange displays of similar-looking books, so make sure your inspiration comes from designs currently on sale. If you feel your designer has come up with something that looks dated, don't accept it. Fashions change not only with regard to images and colours, but also with typefaces, type sizes, and the positions of titles and author names.

Not all freelance graphic designers have experience in book design. They may be capable of coming up with a good design, but they need to understand the technical aspects of allowing for bleeds; allowing for the crease on a paperback cover; allowing for the distance a hardback jacket needs to wrap around the edge; creating and placing a bar code on the design; understanding the spine width required; and many other skills. Make sure your chosen designer has experience in book production, as mistakes will cost you in terms of delay and additional expenses at the printing stage.

The spine width can only be established once the total number of pages is known, i.e. after the typesetting is complete, and once you know the type of paper the printer will use to print the book. Any book printer will tell you the spine width based on those two factors, but check if the number they tell you is the thickness of the book block (the total thickness of the inside pages of the book) or the book block plus the thickness of the cover. The cover on a paperback adds about half a millimetre to the spine width. If it's a hardback, you'll need to take account also of the thickness of the board and the curvature of the paper. It's a complex calculation and there's nothing better than sticking bits of paper together with glue and wrapping them around books of identical size to be certain you have the right measurements.

How do I obtain an ISBN and a bar code?

ISBN STANDS FOR 'International Standard Book Number' (therefore it is tautologous to speak of an 'ISBN number'). An ISBN is a unique code which enables every book in print to be identified unambiguously. Until recently ISBNs have consisted of ten digits, but the number of books published globally since the introduction of the system has used up all of the available combinations, so a new thirteen-digit system has been introduced to allow sufficient unique numbers for many years to come.

A thirteen-digit ISBN consists of a prefix that identifies the publisher, followed by a number that identifies the publisher's book, and a check digit at the end that is generated by an algorithm.

There is no legal obligation to have an ISBN for your book, as it is merely a product number, but without one you can't generate a bar code and you won't be able to sell your book through third-party companies such as bookshops. ISBNs are issued in the UK and Ireland by Nielsen BookData. It isn't possible to buy just one ISBN, so you'll have to buy ten numbers if you want to publish your own book. Having the spare numbers means you'll be ready to publish more books if your first one takes off.

The UK ISBN Agency can be contacted at the following address:

ISBN Agency
3rd Floor
Midas House
62 Goldsworth Road
Woking
Surrey
GU21 6LQ

Tel: 0870 777 8712
Fax: 0870 777 8714
E-mail: isbn@nielsenbookdata.co.uk

www.nbdrs.com/isbn_agency.htm

This is the thirteen-digit ISBN of this edition of this book: 978-1-84024-519-6

978-1-84024 identifies Summersdale. All of the current output of Summersdale books include this number as part of their ISBNs.

519 identifies this book amongst Summersdale's list. Summersdale began in 1990 with an allocation of one hundred ISBNs. When these were used up it purchased a list of 1,000 numbers, of which this book is the 519th to be published.

6 is the check digit.

The creation of a bar code is something your printer or typesetter should be able to do for you. All they need in order to generate it is your ISBN. The bar code should always be on the back cover of the book so that it's easy for the bookshop staff to find it. When they scan the bar code at the till point, it reads the lines in the code which tells the computer system your book's ISBN. The ISBN identifies your book in the shop's database, displays the correct price on the till and records the sale. The computer system then adjusts its inventory record automatically so that the manager can produce a report to show which books have sold and which books to reorder. ISBNs and bar codes streamline the whole operation of bookselling, making it more efficient and ensuring that when a book sells out it isn't forgotten about.

Is a bar code necessary?

There's nothing to stop you publishing a book without a bar code, but it will limit your sales options. High street bookshop chains can stock books without bar codes but they don't like to, because it means they have to create, print and stick a bar code onto the back cover of your book. It's extra work for them, it's messy, and it might cover up important selling points on your book cover.

How do I set the selling price?

SETTING THE OPTIMUM selling price of a book is an art that publishers always strive to perfect. Set it high and you'll have a whopping profit margin on each copy sold, but chances are you'll sell very few copies. Set it low and you might sell in greater numbers but with little or no profit on each copy. Note that I wrote that with a low price you 'might sell' more copies: nothing is guaranteed in the book world, and if the product isn't right for the market, you'll even struggle to give them away for free.

As a publisher I sometimes have excess stock of books that were printed some years ago. Sales of these books through the normal high street bookshops have dropped to negligible levels. One option open to me is to sell the books to high discount shops via remainder dealers who specialise in selling the remainder of a print run cheaply once the initial demand for a title has fallen away. Typically a book would be remaindered at about five or ten per cent of its cover price. But it's not possible to remainder all unwanted stock: certain titles won't sell at any price and there is no option other than to pulp them.

There are rules for setting book prices. They are vague and imprecise, but they should point you in the right direction:

1. Will it be hardback or paperback? Paperbacks are usually cheaper.

2. What are the dimensions and page count? It's hard to justify a high price for a book with few pages.

3. How heavy will it be? There are different kinds of paper available for printing books, and some are much heavier than others. Customers subconsciously weigh books in their hands to get a feel for whether it's worth the money. Two books with identical page sizes and page counts can have different weights according to the papers used.

4. What is the target market for the book? Children's books are cheaper than adult books. Humour books are cheaper than serious books. Fiction is usually relatively cheap, also, because it's aimed at a mass market. Academic books are more expensive than anything else.

5.   What are the prices of the books with which you aim to compete? You should aim to price your book with the rival products in mind.

6.   What is the nearest price point to the figure you have in mind? A price point is a rounded sum, usually close to the value of a currency note but with a penny dropped off to make it sound cheaper. Common cash-related price points therefore occur in multiples of five, but books are often priced at any of the points in-between:

£1.99   *This is rare. When greetings cards cost this much a book should always cost more.*

£2.99   *Forget £2.50 (why lose 49 valuable pennies on every sale?) – this is the lowest amount at which you should price a book. Suitable for tiny 'stocking filler' books.*

£3.99   *Good price point for small books.*

£4.99   *Good price point.*

£5.99   *Common price for paperback fiction and non-fiction.*

£6.99   *Common price for paperback fiction and non-fiction.*

£7.99   *Common price for paperback fiction and non-fiction.*

£8.99	*Less common price – many publishers prefer to jump to the next one.*
£9.99	*Good price point, especially for smaller-size hardbacks.*
£10.99	*Have you ever seen a book at this price? I've published over 500 books, and only one of them was £10.99.*
£11.99	*Less common price – many prefer to jump to the next one.*
£12.99	*Very common price point for medium-size hardbacks.*
£13.99	*Less common price – many prefer to jump to the next one.*
£14.99	*Good price point for larger-size hardbacks.*
£15.99	*Good price point for larger-size hardbacks.*
£16.99	*Good price point for larger-size hardbacks.*
£17.99	*Good price point for larger-size hardbacks.*
£18.99	*Good price point for larger-size hardbacks.*
£19.99	*Good price point for larger-size hardbacks.*
£20.99	*Have you ever seen a book at this price?*
£21.99	*Fairly unusual price.*
£22.99	*Good price point for larger-size hardbacks.*
£23.99	*Fairly unusual price.*
£24.99	*Good price point for larger-size hardbacks.*
£25.99	*Fairly unusual price.*

The list is just a general indication of how many publishers commonly price their books. If you have a substantial academic book or a beautiful coffee table book of glossy photographs you could justifiably price your book much higher.

Selling advertising space in your book

Magazines and newspapers sell advertising space, so why not books? It's rare, but it happens. I've published books in which enough advertising space was sold to cover the entire print costs. It takes a lot of effort to achieve this, and it isn't suitable for every type of book, but in cases where the subject matter is a good match for some companies then it's worth a try. I've had success selling advertising space in cookery books to food manufacturers, for instance, and selling space in travel books to travel agents. Advertising in a book is more permanent and prestigious than advertising in a disposable monthly publication. Remember to emphasise the permanence of the advertising space you're trying to sell. On the negative side, book sales are hard to predict. Newspaper and magazine advertisers know the circulation they can expect. Not only will your book sales be small compared to that, you have no idea exactly how small they will be.

Creating a PDF of the insides and the cover

THE FINAL STAGE of preparing a book for printing is the creation of PDFs. These can be output from design software and will show the precise page and cover layouts, plus printer's marks just off the edges of the pages. Printer's marks are there to identify the document and to show them where to crop the edge of the page. If you are using designers, printers or a self-publishing company, then this isn't a stage you need to worry about. Just insist that the finished PDFs are e-mailed to you for checking (or supplied on a CD if the files are too big to e-mail). This is your last chance to spot errors before the book changes from the virtual production line to the real thing.

The cover of the book should have a separate PDF from the insides. This is because it will be printed separately, sometimes in a different factory.

If you attempt to output your own PDFs, you need to ensure that the settings are correct. Some PDF-making software will attempt to compress your book to save file space and speed up Internet download times. This will result in a poor quality printed result. Maximum quality and minimal or no compression should be used for print-ready

PDFs. There are dozens of settings that could cause problems at this stage but all you need to do is send the PDFs to your printer for checking. They will use software to run automatic 'pre-flight' checks on the files which will highlight any issues that need attention.

Are there any legal implications involved in publishing a book?

WHAT YOU PRINT has to be acceptable within the laws of your country. Certain kinds of pornographic images may be illegal. You also need to be aware of the risk of being accused of plagiarism by other authors if you have based your work or parts of it too closely upon someone else's. Even if you have changed the words you might be guilty of plagiarism if the structure of your story or argument tightly follows theirs.

Libel is another issue to be aware of. If you refer to real people in your book in a manner that unfairly stains their reputation then you're liable to be sued. If you believe your damning portrayal of someone is justified because it's true then you had better be in possession of evidence of that truth.

Quoting from other copyrighted materials is a bit of a grey area. The law allows the reproduction of insubstantial portions of writings, but where to draw the line is not easy to decide. If you take ten words from a novel then it's probably 'insubstantial', but take ten words from a poem or a song and it's a different situation entirely. You can, of course, take your chances, print what you want and hope for the best. The chances that a copyright owner or someone with a financial interest in that person's work will actually come across your book, read it and notice it are almost minuscule in a book that sells a thousand copies. But if your book becomes a hit then you might have trouble sleeping at night, as you lie awake wondering when a letter from litigation lawyers will arrive.

The safe route is to ask for permission to use an extract of text or lyric in your book. Write a letter to the publisher concerned stating precisely the words you would like to quote, the title of the work they come from, and describe the book you plan to publish, including its print run. It's worth specifying that your book is a low budget, self-financed project which is unlikely to sell many copies and that you would respectfully ask that they grant permission for no fee, just a credit on the copyright page. Sometimes you get what you ask for.

If the work you want to quote from is fairly old it might be out of copyright. Copyright in books lasts for seventy years after the death of the author. The laws relating to songs are different at the time of writing, but may be subject to change. Once the copyright expires it cannot be renewed except by special Act of Parliament, and this has only happened once in the case of the rights to *Peter Pan* which have been extended in order to generate an ongoing income for the children's hospital to whom the author bequeathed his royalties. So you can be confident that if an author died more than seventy years ago you will have no problems quoting or reprinting as much of their work as you like. There's nothing to stop you, in fact, reprinting someone's entire book. You don't have to self-publish your own book, you could simply find a forgotten classic and reprint it without needing permission or having to pay royalties.

When your book is published you are obliged by law to provide a small number of copies free of charge to the national libraries so that it may be preserved for posterity.

Legal deposit libraries

Anyone who publishes a book in the UK and Ireland must send copies of that book at their own expense to six libraries where they will form part of the national archive. These libraries are often referred to as copyright libraries or the Legal Deposit Libraries. They receive, free of charge, a copy of every work published in the United Kingdom and the Republic of Ireland.

Five of the six libraries collect their books via a single agency acting on their behalves, so you only need to send a box of five books to that agency and they will pass your books on to the following libraries:

Bodleian Library, Oxford
Cambridge University Library
National Library of Scotland
Library of Trinity College Dublin
National Library of Wales

The address for the agency is:
Agency for the Legal Deposit Libraries
100 Euston Street
London
NW1 2HQ
Tel: 020 7388 5061
Fax: 020 7383 3540

The sixth library is **The British Library**. This has its own Legal Deposit Office to which you must send one copy of your book directly:

Legal Deposit Office
The British Library
Boston Spa
Wetherby
West Yorkshire
LS23 7BY

Don't think you can get away with avoiding a provision of free copies for legal deposit just because you're self-publishing. You will be tracked down via the address registered with your book's ISBN and instructed to send the books. If your print run is small it can be frustrating to give away six copies, but it's an expense you have to plan for. However, the books you send them do not have to be in pristine condition. If you have some copies that are mildly scuffed or scratched there's no reason why you shouldn't use those copies to send to the legal deposit libraries.

You should post your books to the addresses above within a month of publication, preferably immediately on publication, to ensure that you meet the requirements of the law and to avoid the unpleasant scenario of discovering you've sold out before remembering to send your legal deposit copies and then having to reprint the book just to meet your legal obligations.

Currently if you only publish an eBook with no printed edition you don't need to submit anything to the legal deposit libraries, but this situation is being reviewed by government and may change.

How do I choose a print run?

ALL BOOK PUBLISHERS face a frustrating dilemma every time they print a new title. The more copies they print, the cheaper each copy becomes. Therefore the profit margin is potentially greater. But if not all of the books sell, then that profit margin is eaten away by paying for unsold books. Striking a balance between printing too many and printing too few is a skill that publishers always try to perfect.

Here's an example of how the unit cost reduces as the print run increases (the prices indicate the principle rather than the precise cost of a particular book):

Print run	Unit cost
1	£30.00
100	£7.50
500	£4.50
1,000	£2.75
2,500	£2.00
5,000	£1.40
10,000	£0.89
20,000	£0.75

The reduction in the unit cost becomes less as the print run increases. It isn't possible for the savings to continue at the same rate, otherwise the publisher would end up getting them for free if they printed sufficient numbers. Mainstream publishers obtain orders from shops in advance of printing their books, which removes some of the guesswork in deciding quantities. But they don't just print a number to match the total pre-orders. What about reorders from shops after they've sold their initial stock? What about new orders from shops that hadn't ordered the first time around? What about setting aside a quantity of stock for trade samples, review copies and mail order sales?

Publishers use a rule of thumb to set their print runs, based on a multiple of the advance orders. Typically this will be a factor of three. Get a hundred advance orders and print three hundred books. Get a thousand advance orders and print three thousand. The idea is not to have to reprint the book too soon, and not to have stock that sits in a warehouse for decades. A couple of years' worth of stock is ideal. When self-publishing it's likely that the stock will sit somewhere in your house, cluttering your living space, so ensuring that you don't overestimate your stock requirements is even more important.

Most of the hundreds of authors whom I helped to publish their own books over the years chose print runs between five hundred and a thousand units. Some chose to print just fifty or one hundred books. These authors stood no chance of making a profit from their venture. Their aim was to create enough copies for themselves, their friends and their families. To earn your investment back from book sales you normally need to sell about a thousand copies. That's just enough to break even. To make a profit, you need to sell more. These numbers are very approximate and will obviously vary according to the print cost of the book, its selling price, the trade discounts given and other costs that may be associated with the book, such as paying for the use of images from photo libraries.

How do I choose a printer?

YOUR LOCAL PRINT shop is unlikely to be able to produce bound books like this one. Book printing is as much a manufacturing process as it is a printing process. Book printers are specialists – you won't find them printing leaflets and business cards on the side.

The machinery needed for book printing is expensive, and not all machines can handle all kinds of books. The result is that each printing firm has a range of book sizes and types that it can produce. The range is pretty wide for most of them, but when dealing with the extremes of big and small books, colour work and unusual types of paper, you may have to look further to find the right printer. Most mass-produced colour books are printed abroad: China, India and parts of Europe commonly offer competitive prices.

Get printing quotes from as many printers as you can. Any money saved at this stage means fewer books will have to be sold to break even. There are too many UK book printers to list here, but you can find them all on one handy website: www.selectprinter.com.

Print on demand

There is an alternative to sticking your finger in the wind and trying to guess how many copies you'll sell. Instead of gambling on a print run of one or two thousand copies, consider whether your book is suited to print on demand. To print in this way entails setting up your book files with a print on demand company, such as Lightning Source or Lulu.com. Your book is listed on websites such as Amazon and can be ordered by any bookshop. When an order is placed, it is sent electronically to the print on demand company. They print a copy of the book from the PDFs you supplied them. They then deliver the book to the shop that placed the order and issue an invoice on your behalf. When payment is received, they pass on a share of the money to you, the publisher.

It's an efficient way of avoiding the need to tie up your money in stock (and keeps your living space uncluttered). It also ensures that your book need never go out of print. There's a catch, of course, and that's the price you pay per copy printed. It's higher than when you print a thousand or so copies. Far higher. In fact, the costs are so high that this kind of printing only becomes cost-effective when the book is highly priced relative to its page count because the price you pay is determined by the number of pages in the book.

Let's say a print on demand company charges a penny a page (black and white only) plus a pound for the cover (full colour). Paperback binding is included in those prices. Your book is a three-hundred-page novel that you want to make available in paperback at £5.99, which is a competitive price compared to other novels on the market. The cost of printing the inside pages will be £3.00 and the cost of the cover adds another £1.00, so that's a total of £4.00 per copy. This amount is £1.99 less than the retail price. Great – nice profit margin. Except there's no margin at all, in reality. Unless you're able to sell the book directly to customers at the full retail price you will have to give a trade discount to retail shops and websites. The average trade discount is almost 50 per cent. Even allowing for the fact that self-publishers sometimes get away with offering smaller discounts such as 35 per cent, that still means the book cannot be sold profitably. And there may be other costs to bear, such as postage. So this method of printing won't work for all self-publishers.

Print on demand has other drawbacks. There is no warehouse holding stock of your book, therefore there is nowhere to which shops can return unsold stock. If a shop knows it can't return your book it may be less likely to order it in the first place.

Poor print quality used to be an issue with print on demand, but books printed that way these days are usually indistinguishable from bulk-produced titles. But there will be restrictions on the size, binding and paper types that are available to you. Your book will have to be made from a set of standard ingredients so that it can be printed quickly and automatically.

Some things to avoid when printing a book...

Don't insist on your own design ideas against the advice of professionals

Never choose A5 or A4 as the size of your book

Never choose a type of card for the front cover which is glossy on the inside

What can a self-publishing company do for me?

MOST OF THE effort and responsibility can be taken off your shoulders when you hire the services of a self-publishing company. They will take care of the cover design, typesetting, scanning and manipulation of any images you supply to them, acquisition of an ISBN and a bar code, and printing. Most self-publishing companies are not printers – they won't print your book themselves. But they will be familiar with the best printing firm to do your kind of book and will act on your behalf in arranging the printing for you.

There are, however, printing firms that offer self-publishing services as a sideline. The company I used to co-run was a sideline to a mainstream publishing business, so we were able to offer our spare capacity and skills to self-publishing authors. Every book project that came along was different. We offered authors the opportunity to create books in any size and format, on any subject, any print run. There were so many variations in what an author might require that we had to quote for every job individually. In contrast, some self-publishing companies offer very few options in an attempt to simplify and standardise the process, which also has a cost benefit. Be sure that this approach won't compromise your book's chances of commercial success before going down this route. A generic cover design that's also on the front of dozens of other books, all unrelated except for the use of the same self-publishing service, might not do you any favours.

Whichever company you use, don't think you can just leave it to them and sit at home until your beautiful books arrive. Some self-publishing companies are run by people with little experience of commercial book publishing and they get away with producing books that are poorly typeset and badly designed because most authors are so blinded by the thrill of seeing their name in print that they don't notice.

This is why it's important to look at examples of previous books that they have produced on behalf of self-publishing authors and to check for the layout problems listed later in this book.

What happens if I spot an error in my book after it has been printed?

THIS IS, SADLY, very common. The severity of the problem can be major – such as a spelling mistake in the title on the front cover (sounds impossible but I've seen it happen). Or it could be something very small, such as a missing apostrophe in the middle of the book. Sometimes the pages are in the wrong order or the words run off the edge of the page.

The first thing to remember is that mistakes happen to all publishers. It's extremely rare for a book to be printed without a single mistake, and that goes for the largest publishers who have huge editorial teams whose job it is to make sure these things don't happen. They do. Producing a book is a complex task. Even the process of fixing errors found prior to printing is fraught with risk: if the typesetter is asked to change a word it's possible that a slip of the finger on the mouse could cause a whole line to be deleted at the same time. This could go unnoticed unless you are able to reread the entire book after every stage of correction.

The second thing to do is to identify whether the printer is at fault, or whether you are at fault. Faults under your responsibility include services for which you hired freelancers, such as editing or typesetting. Faults in the text, layout or design are also your responsibility, even if you have hired a self-publishing company to produce the book for you. They will make mistakes, as we all do, but you will have to inspect the book's cover and insides before going to press and, if you've signed it off as being ready for printing, then you have to accept any errors that you failed to spot.

The good news is that if the fault can be traced to the printer then you are entitled to get the books reprinted for free. As the faulty books are of no value whatsoever to the printing company you can usually hang onto them, and if the fault is relatively minor there's nothing to stop you selling those copies once you run out of good stock.

The first copy I took out of the box of the first book I self-published looked perfect until I opened it up. The first thirty-two pages had been repeated twice at the end of the book, and another chunk of thirty-two pages was missing entirely. My heart sank, and I nervously opened up some more copies from the print run of one thousand. Fortunately all of the others were fine. By a thousand-to-one chance I had picked out the only faulty copy from the print run. The printer had made an error in binding one copy.

Some lessons need to be learned from this:

1. Printers make mistakes. They do their best to weed out faulty books before delivering them to you, but since book manufacturing is done mainly by machinery, it's impossible to check every copy individually (unless you want to pay twice as much for the stock). Therefore in every print run you should expect a small amount of spoilage. It could be a printing error, which means too much or not enough ink on the page. It could be a binding error, where pages are in the

incorrect order, missing, or duplicated, or a binding error involving the cover being glued on in slightly the wrong position so that the spine text isn't centred accurately. It could be a trimming error, where the guillotine used to trim the edges of the book is set at the wrong position and the books are trimmed at a weird angle, or too big or too small. Some trimming errors result in pages being stuck together at the top (where the giant sheets of paper have been folded to make smaller pages but not cut in the right place). It could be a transit problem, which is as simple as a box of books getting dropped causing damage to the stock or rainwater penetrating the box and soaking the books inside.

2. You should always flick through a book before sending it to a reviewer or mail order customer, just in case it's suffered from a printing or binding problem, and you should always expect that occasionally a customer will return a book to you complaining that it's faulty.

Errata slips

If an error exists in the printed book that is your fault but you don't want to pay for a reprint, a simple solution is to print little errata slips listing the page and line number and the correct text. These slips can either be placed loose inside the front cover of each copy, glued in place, or printed on stickers and stuck on. Despite the fairly high incidence of errors in books, most authors choose not to use errata slips because they don't want to draw attention to mistakes that perhaps might otherwise go unnoticed.

There are certain errors where errata slips are essential. Take the example of a recipe book in which the quantity of an ingredient reaches unhealthy levels due to a typing error. Or a novel in which the wrong character name appears at a crucial moment, thus altering the intended story fundamentally – you wouldn't want the bad guy riding off into the sunset with the heroine instead of the good guy, would you? What if your book is about health and the word 'not' is accidentally included in a statement about products that are harmful to the human body? In such cases the errata slip must be used if the stock is not going to be pulped and the book immediately reprinted.

Note that 'errata' should be used in the heading of the inserted note when listing more than one error; 'erratum' when there is a single error to correct.

Can I fix errors in a reprint?

If you spot an error in your book after it has been printed, but you feel confident that the original print run will sell out, you will have the opportunity to fix the error in a reprint. Don't rush the typesetter to make the corrections because you might find that other errors will surface in the coming weeks as readers send you feedback. You won't have to ask for feedback – usually it comes whether you want it or not, especially if there is an e-mail address in the book for them to contact you directly. Collate all of the corrections you want to make so that they can be entered at the same time into the page layout software and only one new PDF will have to be created.

When reprinting a book, get your typesetter to add 'Reprinted' and the year so that you can easily distinguish between the original edition and the corrected version.

If you've set up your book for print on demand and find a mistake, then the consequences are less severe. Amend your typeset file, or get your typesetter to fix it, and supply a fresh PDF to the print on demand company. However, they may charge you a fee for replacing the file they have in their system. It's not their fault that you made a mistake in the first PDF, after all. Your typesetter may also charge you for making the alteration and the time spent creating the new PDF.

Should I have a launch party and signing sessions?

BY ALL MEANS throw a party. If publishing your book isn't cause for celebration, what is? Hosting your party at a local bookshop is a great way to combine a signing session with a knees-up and the opportunity to cement a relationship with the manager of the best outlet for your book. I've held many launch parties in bookshops, and it means that your book becomes known to all the staff of that shop and is therefore more likely to be kept prominently in stock. If you can persuade the manager that they are likely to sell a worthwhile number of books on the night, they might even allow you to hold the party there for free, provided you pay for the drinks, snacks and promotional advertising.

When arranging a launch party remember to invite local dignitaries, members of clubs and societies (especially reading groups) and local journalists. Give a little speech about your book and make sure that journalists get copies of the book for free. Everyone else pays for it.

Signing sessions away from your home territory are best avoided, though, unless your level of celebrity is sufficient to bring out the crowds. If you want to try, all it takes is to visit or call the respective shop managers with your proposal, send them a copy of the book (or your information sheet if the book is still at the printing presses), and arrange to get an interview on local radio the day before plus a news item in the local paper during the week before. Design some posters and leaflets about the event to display in the shop, and bring enough copies of your book along on the night to be able to satisfy demand. For most of us, sadly, two or three copies should do it.

Shop managers will often hang on to substantial amounts of stock of your book after the event, which you can sign before leaving. Even if the signing event itself is a damp squib, the pile of signed stock will have a reasonable chance of selling through over the coming weeks.

The signing event is unlikely to be just you sitting behind a table with a pile of books on it, signing them quickly for customers who are queuing halfway down the street. That's how superstar authors do it. At the beginner's end of the business it works better if you conduct a reading from your book to an assembled group, give a talk and answer questions. Only once the audience has had a chance to get to know you and your book much better do you announce that you will be signing copies for anyone who wishes to buy one.

How important is it to publicise my book?

PERSUADING A SHOP to stock copies of your book is one thing, but it isn't really a sale until a customer buys it. Until then it could be returned to you. Publishers often face the unpleasant situation wherein having successfully sold their entire print run into the shops they enthusiastically order a reprint to replenish their stocks, only to find that the initial print run starts to get returned, unsold, by the shops. So having placed your book in a number of retail outlets, it's important to let potential customers know that it's there. Sales through casual browsing aren't enough. You will always achieve some sales through this method – we've all bought books on impulse having picked them up out of curiosity in a bookshop – but the best way to get the stock moving is to publicise it. You know you're doing a good job as a publisher when a customer enters a bookshop intent on searching for and buying your book.

So publicity reduces the number of books likely to be returned unsold, but it also generates fresh orders for your book. One way to generate publicity is to hire an advertising firm and pay for billboards and television commercials about your book. These methods will stimulate sales, but when was the last time you saw a book advertised on the telly? The book industry is small compared to soap powder. We all use soap powder, and we buy soap powder products more than once a year. But we don't all buy books. Even amongst the smallish sector of the population that does buy books, very few of them will buy the same book. It simply doesn't pay to advertise your book to the mass market.

There's no harm in the population at large hearing about your book if you don't have to pay for the privilege, though.

Can I publicise my book for free?

Well, it's never entirely free, but it doesn't cost any more than a bit of postage and some complimentary copies of your book. There are thousands of journalists who make a living from writing book reviews (and sometimes from selling the sample books sent to them on eBay!). This industry is there to be exploited, so go ahead. Of course, there's always the risk that a critic will write an unfavourable review, but sometimes even bad publicity can be better than none at all. Some readers buy books that have been the subject of a bad review just so that they can compare their own opinion to that of the critic.

What are uncorrected proof copies?

Some publishers will print a small quantity of their book about six months ahead of the main print run. Advance copies are printed digitally, using the same machines that create print on demand books, and a typical print run would be between fifty and a hundred copies. They are referred to in the trade as 'uncorrected proof copies' because they won't have been through the full editorial process, they will have been typeset quickly and may still contain mistakes. Publishers print them with a disclaimer on the cover saying something like 'Uncorrected proof copy, not for resale, publication date...' so that the edition won't be confused with the final published book and won't find its way onto the retail market.

There are three advantages in printing a small number of your books so far in advance.

Firstly, it's a useful tool for building enthusiasm amongst influential bookshop managers, especially those responsible for making buying decisions across entire chains of stores. Sending the advance copy also to buyers from supermarkets and other potential stockists will increase your chances of getting an order from them. When visiting shops in person it helps to have a physical book to flick through. The managers can visualise more easily the product you want them to buy. If they express sufficient interest and you have a few copies to spare you can leave it with them to read.

The second use for proof copies is in getting reviews published. Professional reviewers don't like to review a bundle of A4 sheets of paper or an e-mailed Word document. They like a proper, bound book that they can easily carry with them and read on the train or on the toilet. If you want them to like you and your writing, you should at least give them something easy to work with. Another thing about reviewers is that they like to be topical because their readers want content that is new all the time. A book that has already been published is old news and they won't be interested in reviewing it. Unless you print advance copies you will have no choice other than trying to persuade them to review your book after it has been published. Actually, there is still one option open to you: the 'official' publication date of your book doesn't have to coincide with the day the stock arrives on your doorstep, hot off the press. You can inform reviewers and the book trade that the publication date is a date up to three months later, for instance. This will enable reviewers to feel confident that they are not wasting their time in delivering old news.

The third advantage is in obtaining review quotes far enough ahead of the publication date of the real book that you can add those quotes to your cover design. Have you ever noticed brand new books appearing in the shops with reviews already printed on their front cover? Unless the reviewer is a personal friend of the author, the odds are that an uncorrected proof copy was sent out to reviewers several months before the final book went to press.

The vast majority of self-published authors will not print uncorrected proof copies. To do so means timetabling their publication process over a longer period. The temptation for authors who are desperately keen to see themselves in print is to arrange for the printing as soon as the writing process is finished. True, they will see themselves in print sooner, but in the long run fewer people will get to read their work because sales will be substantially fewer. Most authors aren't even aware that to gain the most from printing their work they need to view it as a two-stage process. The extra cost is never welcome, nor are the delays. But if you have talent as a writer and you feel that your book deserves the best chance you can give it, then an early printing of at least fifty copies of an uncorrected proof edition will give you a significant advantage over other self-published authors.

How do I get my book reviewed?

WHETHER YOU INTEND to send uncorrected proof copies or the finished product, it's best to start by sending a press release to a list of publications and radio or television shows that you think might be interested in reviewing it. Follow this mailing (or e-mailing) within a week with a phone call asking if anyone there has received the press release and would like to receive a copy of the book. If you get a positive response, send the book immediately. Alternatively, you could simply send unsolicited copies to your selected list of recipients. This is quicker but more expensive.

Magazine reviews

The majority of a typical monthly magazine's content is put together at least three months before the publication date – only news items will be added at the last minute. Book reviews are timed to coincide, where possible, with a book's publication date so that means the review has to be written three months before the publication date. It takes time to read your book, so the reviewer should ideally have at least an extra month on top of that in which to plough through your pages.

Newspaper reviews

Newspaper content is created daily or weekly, but a book reviewer still needs to have enough time to read the book and write something about it, so try to ensure they receive your book about four to six weeks ahead of the publication date.

Website reviews

A quick web search will normally identify dozens of sites that are relevant to your book. It's common for specialist interest websites to feature book reviews or recommendations. Sometimes you can even post the recommendation on the site yourself. If this isn't possible, post a copy of the book to the people behind the site requesting a review and a link to Amazon. The great thing about the Amazon affiliate scheme is that they reward the website with a sales commission for every customer who clicks through and buys something, so it's in their interest to host information about your book on their site.

Amazon review deal

You should expect your friends and family to support your publishing venture, so there's nothing wrong in getting them to pay for their copies of your book. But you can benefit from giving away free copies provided the recipient promises to write a review of your book on Amazon. You shouldn't ask them for fake reviews or unjust praise, just an honest and detailed appraisal of your writing that will help guide other readers. One book given away for free on these terms could generate ten sales on Amazon as a result.

What happens if I get bad reviews?

When you indulge in any creative project that ultimately finds its way into the public domain you are at risk of receiving negative feedback. Whether your work is a painting, a film or a book, members of the public feel they have the right to criticise the artistic efforts put before them. Criticism is always made without any regard to the sensitivity of the artist. It makes no allowances for the courage it takes to expose your creation to the world. It ignores the effort you put in, the genius you possess and the sector of the market for whom your work was intended. If the critic doesn't like it, that's it: out pops a bad review.

Authors are particularly prone to this due to the Amazon review system whereby anyone can write a review about any book, whether or not they've even read it properly, and that review will appear permanently on the website. What frequently happens is that the kind of person that you never thought in a million years would want to read your book actually does so and hates it. They express their hatred of your writing vehemently on the website and the result is that fewer people want to buy your book. The really frustrating thing is that you know, deep inside, that their opinion is unfair or even wrong. It could be that they don't know the subject matter as well as you, or that their taste isn't suited to your book due to their age or cultural background. And what can you do about it? Absolutely nothing. Unless they allow their e-mail address to appear with their review, which is rare in the case of bad reviews, their anonymity is protected. You have no way to answer them back.

The first way of coping with this regrettable side effect of becoming a self-published author is to get a sense of perspective. Everyone is different. We all have different tastes. Not everyone reads *Harry Potter*. Not everyone drives diesel cars. When you wrote your book did you think it would appeal to the whole world? Of course not. If it's aimed at a young adult market, and is full of colourful language (mostly shades of blue), then older readers generally won't appreciate it.

I once had a letter from a lady in her seventies with shaky handwriting who, for some inexplicable reason, had read a travel book I had written for the 17–25 market, *Don't Lean Out of the Window*. Enjoyment of that book depended upon the reader being in tune with a modern, ironic sense of humour and being part of the language culture where swear words have no power whatsoever to offend. University students love it. Pensioners hate it. That's the way it was written. In fact, the first edition was printed with a warning on the cover stating that the book was not suitable for readers over the age of thirty (I removed that warning on subsequent editions when I passed that age bracket myself). So what does that say about the old woman's criticism? It means that her opinion is irrelevant, because I know that someone like her would not enjoy that book and I would never want anyone without a healthy sense of irony to be exposed to such filth. So I don't view my book purely from the perspective of one irrelevant review. I'm fortunate enough to receive frequent e-mails and letters from younger readers who love that book because it connects with them in a way that other books don't. I can be satisfied in my mind that the book does its job, and that anyone who doesn't like it is entitled to that opinion but it isn't relevant if they are not of the appropriate mindset.

Don't think that every book I write is full of foul language, by the way. I got a bad review for *Tish and Pish: How to be of a Speakingness Like Stephen Fry*, which complained that I hadn't used enough swearing. It's hard to win sometimes.

Newspaper and magazine extracts

Extracts work differently to reviews, and both of those differences work in your favour. You get paid for extracts. Newspapers and magazines have to pay contributing writers for the words that fill their publications, and if they fill two or three pages with text and perhaps illustrations or photos from your book, then you will be paid for that. The level of payment varies from a small token payment from specialist magazines with low circulations to very high payments from national newspapers for extracts of celebrity biographies containing profound personal revelations that will sell more copies at the news-stands. Just because a newspaper offers to buy extract rights from you doesn't mean you'll necessarily earn big bucks, though. The majority of these deals are done for modest amounts of money.

The other thing about extracts is that they are neutral about your book. You won't get an extract with scathing comments about your turgid prose. The extract will speak for itself and you can rest assured that no one at the newspaper will write anything grossly unfair.

Always ask for a photo of your book cover to be printed together with its title, price, publisher name and publication date. Newspaper editors like to disguise book extracts as news articles and if you don't ask for these things you won't get them. If it is available for sale on your personal website try to get the site address listed. Some publications will include an order form at the end of the extract so that readers can buy the book. Often this will involve a third-party order fulfilment company who will take a slice of the pie, but if you can get the orders to come directly to you then your profit margin is increased considerably.

What do I do if someone wants me for a broadcast interview about my book?

If a researcher calls you to discuss a possible appearance try to talk incessantly to them. That's what they're testing you for. Obviously you shouldn't ramble on irrelevantly and impolitely, but give full and detailed, chatty answers to any of their questions to give them confidence that you would be a worthwhile guest. They're not going to look good to their employers if a guest comes on the show and mumbles monosyllabic answers. A good interview is one where the presenter uses hardly any of the prepared questions, so prove to them on the phone that you're a good talker and they'll be keen to book you.

How do I get local radio interviews?

Local radio stations, both BBC and independent, are usually kind to authors in their area. They don't distinguish between published and self-published authors. Anyone from their region with a new book to talk about is usually worth getting on the show. A simple phonecall to your local stations, or mailing them a press release and a copy of the book, is usually all it takes. It really is as simple as that.

Local radio is extremely influential on local book sales. All of the listeners buy their books from a small group of shops in the area. You won't get much advance notice of a radio interview, but try to persuade the local booksellers to stock up on copies of your book before you go on air.

How do I get national radio interviews?

National radio interview opportunities are more limited. The procedure for getting them is the same, but the chances of getting on a particular show are much smaller. Make a list of all the national radio shows that feature interviews with authors, find out the names of the producers of each one, the contact them all by telephone, e-mail or mail with a press release and a copy of the book.

As with local radio, you probably won't have much time between sending them the press release and appearing on air, so make sure you don't send your press releases out to any radio shows until your book is in the shops.

How do I give a good radio interview?

Radio interviews are technically simple to conduct because it doesn't matter what you look like or what you look at. You can even smuggle notes in to remind yourself of the main points of your argument. Avoid gesticulation when talking excitedly about your book – I've whacked many a microphone mid-interview in this way. Don't lean in towards the microphone, because the engineer will have set the audio levels to record you from a comfortable seated position.

Listen to the question that the presenter asks you, but don't feel you have to stick rigidly to the angle they choose. Politicians are expert at ignoring a question and simply saying what they want to say, and in a more polite way you can do the same. Decide in advance of the interview what points you want to get across and twist your answers in a direction that suits you. Have anecdotes ready, have your book in front of you with crucial pages marked in case you have to look at them and read something out.

Local radio presenters won't usually read your book: any questions they ask you will be based on the blurb they've read and any sales points you mention in the press release you sent them. This keeps the interview at a relatively light and fluffy level and won't challenge you too much. Presenters on national radio shows can be a little more hard-hitting in their interviews, but the effect on sales makes it worth going a few rounds with them.

How can I get local television interviews?

Local television rarely offers chat show opportunities, but the daily news shows are always hungry for quirky stories about things that people have done in the region. Publishing your own book isn't news in itself: every day dozens of people do it in every county. What can turn your book into a worthwhile news item is its context. Have you overcome personal tragedy or hardship to achieve this goal? Is the book related to a topical event? Has it caused controversy? Are you going to do a publicity stunt that will provide them with interesting video footage to illustrate the piece? Is there a celebrity connected to the book? Elements such as these will enhance your chances of getting your book promoted for free on local television.

If they want to run a story about you it will be within a day or two of them finding out about it, so again make sure they don't hear anything about you until the book is in the shops. Potential customers will only search for your book once after they've seen you on television. If the book doesn't reach the shops for a week after the interview then that publicity will have been wasted.

How can I get national television interviews?

Obtaining free book promotion on national television is not as hard as it sounds. It's simply a matter of letting the producers of every relevant show know about you and your book, and if the combination of you and your book excites them then you might get on the show. Don't tell them too soon – these shows tend to be live and have a fairly short lead time, sometimes just a matter of a couple of days. They like to be topical and if they want you on the show it will usually be as soon as possible, so make sure you actually have your book printed before you tell them about it.

I got my first television appearances from sending a simple faxed press release to about ten different chat shows. What happened next was so fast it was surreal: one weekend I was sitting on my sofa at home watching a prime time Saturday night chat show on BBC 1; the next weekend I was on the show myself together with a bunch of celebrities. It was faster than I had expected, and the book was still at the presses, so I glued a dummy cover onto a completely different book. The presenter pretended to be leafing through it during the interview and the audience of ten million was none the wiser. It was a shame the books weren't in the shops at that point!

Getting television slots like this is a little easier if you have a website profiling you and a showreel on DVD or as a downloadable video file to prove that you can talk coherently, but it's not essential. If your book is non-fiction then you are going to be perceived as an expert in your subject, and you will probably find that from time to time you get approached by television and radio shows out of the blue wanting you to be a guest expert.

How do I give a good television interview?

Television interviews are much more intimidating than radio. The production crew is bigger, the lights are brighter, and instead of a friendly-looking fluffy microphone in front of you there's an evil-looking, Dalek-like television camera trying to see into your soul. Television certainly takes some getting used to, but there are a few basic points to remember:

1. Concentrate on breathing in and out, deeply and slowly, in the seconds before the interview begins. This will calm your nerves.

2. Forget about the millions who might be watching. Just engage in a conversation with

the presenter and with fellow guests where required.

3. Never look at the camera unless you're asked to read an autocue, which is very unlikely, or unless there's a phone-in, in which case you must look at the camera if someone phones in to speak to you. Otherwise keep your eyes and your attention focused on the presenter.

4. Remember to carry a copy of your book onto the set with you. Don't trust the producer who tells you in the green room before the show that everything is sorted and a copy of the book will be with the presenter. They might be lying in order to prevent a blatant book plug, so bring your own copy with you onto the set and place it prominently, facing the cameras rather than facing you.

5. Be lively and enthusiastic about your book. Mention the title at least twice and try to pitch its merits as you would to anyone you meet who enquires about it.

6. Don't be offended when you realise that the presenter hasn't read your book. I've given

more than forty television interviews about my books, and the only presenters I was certain had actually read the books were Richard and Judy.

Should I plug my book blatantly?

Of course, that's why you're there. Some presenters will do it for you, but don't count on it. Producers are nervous about getting into trouble for excessive product promotion and will ask their presenters not to mention book titles or show book covers clearly. Television shows have been fined on occasions for too much plugging of commercial products, but you as a guest don't have to worry about that. Your job is to mention your book's title in as many of the answers you give during the interview as you can.

For instance, if the interviewer asks why you wrote your book, don't start your response with 'Because...'. Start your answer with 'I wrote [TITLE OF BOOK] because...'.

Should I get a fee for appearing on a show?

Not usually. Most shows will pay reasonable expenses but they'll argue that your contribution doesn't deserve a fee because you'll benefit from increased book sales, which is fair enough. If that's the line they take then it's vital to plug your book shamelessly. Occasionally the format of the show will make a plug almost impossible, and in those circumstances it's acceptable to ask for a modest fee. As you become more experienced at expert appearances you may reach a position of minor celebrity which will justify asking for a fee for all appearances, but this will take some time to achieve.

Competition prizes and giveaways

It's very common for publications and local radio stations to publicise your book for free in return for being able to offer a few copies of your book as a prize for their readers or listeners. The copies given away cost you very little, and you're guaranteed favourable comments about the book because no one is going to offer as a prize a product that they have slated.

Advertising

This should be carefully targeted. It's not normally sensible to advertise a book for sale in a national newspaper. Even the mainstream publishers rarely do that. You need to find a publication or a geographical area which serves a concentration of your potential book buyers. Be warned that even a book on fishing advertised in a fishing magazine may not generate enough sales to cover the costs of the advert. Advertising is difficult to get right.

A one-off placement might not work because it might take a reader several issues to notice it. You'll lose sales if you're unable to accept credit cards. You'll lose sales if the advert has no impact or is otherwise poorly designed. Full-page magazine adverts can cost as much as your entire print run of books, so it's best only to go down the paid advertising route when all options of getting it plugged for free have been exhausted.

With a little advance planning you might be able to persuade a magazine or newspaper editor to swap advertising space with you. One page at the back of your book could be worth a page in their publication. No one can lose out with that kind of a deal.

How do I go about selling my book?

LET'S BEGIN WITH some grossly unfair generalisations about authors. They are introverts. They like to lock themselves away for thousands of hours while they write. The rest of the world goes about its business, but writers just sit at home and write. When they finally emerge, blinking, into the daylight clutching their newly self-published masterpiece, they don't know how to sell it. They barely know how to relate to other humans. OK, this is an exaggeration, but the point is that writing skills and sales skills are not often found in the same person. Car salesmen don't usually make the best writers, and writers would starve if they had to sell cars for a living.

So how can a self-published author sell enough books to earn back their investment if they have no more experience of selling than a Sunday morning spent at a car boot sale? It comes down to planning. You don't need to be a great salesperson to sell your print run. Plan every stage of your self-publishing adventure and the book should, at least to some extent, sell itself. Here's how.

You're going to write lists of potential buyers for your book. That includes friends and family. Forget about giving them free copies. They'll be happy to support you by paying for their books, especially as they'll be getting signed copies, and they'll value their copies more if they pay for them anyway. Your list will include organisations, publications, websites and businesses. It will be a thorough analysis of everyone and everywhere that could conceivably contribute to your sales figures. Let's look at them in more detail.

Friends and family

Create a mailing list of friends and family to whom you can send a leaflet about your book. The leaflet doesn't have to be too fancy, but it should include a colour reproduction of the book's cover design, the blurb, plus a simple tear-off order form. It should NOT offer the book at a discount. Your book's selling price has been set by you at a level that reflects what the book is worth. Let your friends pay a fair price for it. They should also be charged for postage and packaging. You have a long way to go to recoup your investment and you can't afford to give away money at this stage. Some of your friends might prefer to buy your book from a shop or from Amazon, but you should discourage this because it would halve the amount you would receive from the sale. Besides, they get added value by ordering from you because they get signed copies.

Social Networking Sites

Once you've exhausted the friends and family listed in your address book it's time to get creative. Have a look online at Friends Reunited, Facebook and MySpace. Look up your old friends, schools, colleges and places of work. How many hundreds of names are there on these sites for your school? How many of them might remember you? It doesn't really matter if you think you can't even remember them. Join the sites so that you can contact them and tell everyone with whom you may ever have come into contact about your book. Write entries about yourself on the sites and mention your book there.

Organisations

Clubs, societies, associations and other kinds of interest-related organisations have mailing lists of their members. Any organisation of which you are a member will normally be happy to support you in your efforts to sell your book, especially if the subject matter is relevant to the club's activities. Don't be shy in asking for their help. Put up a poster on their noticeboard. Write an article for their newsletter and provide an order form for the book. If the club is affiliated to similar clubs in other parts of the country or to other branches of the same organisation, try to get some national coverage through their publications. I helped an author to self-publish a book about her travels. She was a member of the Rotary Club and she found that support for the book came not just from her local branch but from all over the country.

Local shops

Support for self-publishing authors has traditionally been strong amongst small, independent shops. My first self-published book was stocked by traders all over my local town: all I had to do was turn up with a briefcase full of books and some order forms and many shop managers would simply order on the spot and take stock from my bag. Some even paid me in cash from their till. When approaching local shops you don't need to restrict yourself to bookshops. Newsagents, garden centres, gift shops and specialist stores will sometimes stock self-published books. It's important for you to back up their good faith in taking your book by generating local publicity that will enable them to sell their copies.

National shops

It takes a serious effort to persuade shops across the country to stock your book. You're up against all kinds of obstacles, aside from the obvious geographical problem of only being able to visit a small number of shops in one day. In this technological age it seems a bit old-fashioned to be talking about visiting shops in person in order to make a sale, but shop managers respond positively to that personal touch, the tactile experience of holding your book or dummy book in their hands, and the persuasive pressure you can exert on them. It's easier to ignore an e-mail or an order form that comes in the post than to ignore someone standing in front of you. Forget about trying to sell to them by telephone, by the way. Bookshops are busy places and you can spend hours just waiting for someone to pick up the phone.

So there's nothing better than a face-to-face meeting with a buyer from a bookshop. The problem is that they operate strict appointment diaries which limit the number of publishers' representatives that they see in a day. The small number of appointment slots that are available will be booked up many months in advance by professional sales reps who visit these shops all the time. If that wasn't bad enough, you'll find that even if a slot is available on the day you want to visit, the moment you say the name of your self-published imprint the response is very likely to be 'Oh, I don't think we're allowed to see you. You're not on the list.' The list they're talking about is a fairly short list of approved publishers' representatives, each of whom will be showing a large number of new books on every visit. They won't make space in the diary for someone with only one book. Even though you know you can show it to them in less than thirty seconds, they won't want to know. Profit margins for high street book retailers are narrow and the more reps they see the fewer staff they have available for dealing with customers, hence the continuing squeeze on the number of reps they will allow into the shop.

This situation leaves you with a few options, however.

1.   Try guerrilla repping techniques. Get your information sheet, book, order form and delivery notes at the ready and turn up, unannounced, in each bookshop. Find a staff member who isn't too busy to talk to you, and try your luck. With the major chains you will probably get more rejections than successes. WHSmith branch level staff have no buying powers, so don't waste your time visiting these shops. Only deal with WHSmith at head office level. Policies in bookshops change over time with regard to reps who appear out of the ether in this manner: you'll find hardened staff who will angrily eject you

immediately and you'll find sympathetic staff who will try their best to help you get your publishing business off the ground. The overall level of success you experience with this method of selling will depend on the genre of your book, the quality and style of its cover design and printed format, and on your interpersonal skills. If you can accept repeated rejection and still face the next shop with a smile, then you have what it takes!

2. Contact freelance sales representatives and try to persuade them to show your book to the shops along with all the other ones they carry. This won't be easy to achieve for a publisher with just one title, as it's not cost effective for them to deal with you, but if the book is strong enough and they think they might get a bestseller on their hands, then you could get lucky. Be aware that freelance sales reps will take a percentage of the invoice value not just of the orders they take directly, but of all reorders from the same shop. Often they will expect a percentage of all sales from within their defined territory, regardless of whether they were involved in the sale or not.

3. Deal with the head office of every bookshop chain. You might not get an appointment to see anyone, and you certainly can't turn up on spec and expect to be seen, but they will respond to mailings, e-mails and phone calls. Waterstone's has a buyer at head office level who is dedicated to dealing only with small publishers. They don't want to miss out on anything that might be important just because it was self-published.

4. Print a leaflet about your book with an order form included, and mail it to bookshops nationally. A list of every bookshop in the UK is published by the Bookseller's Association every year, and the information is available on their website: www.booksellers.org.uk. They will even sell you sheets of preprinted bookshop address labels to speed up the mailing process.

5. Use wholesalers. The big book wholesalers – Gardners, Bertrams and Total Home Entertainment (THE) – each have teams of reps who service independent bookshops. These companies provide a sales, ware-housing, dispatch and invoicing service and

are an effective means of reaching any bookshop in the country. They don't necessarily want to stock every self-published book, however. You might need to persuade them that you have plans to grow your publishing list, as they can be reluctant to sign a publisher with just one title.

6. Use a distributor. Book distribution companies are essentially warehouses with reactive invoicing and dispatch facilities. They tend not to offer proactive sales services, so you would need to find another means of obtaining orders in the first place. Distributors take care of the hassle of posting books, creating invoices and chasing payment. But again, you're at a disadvantage with just one book. Few distributors are likely to want to take on a single book, although they will take you more seriously if you have convincing plans to publish regularly. I managed to get a distributor to sign me up even though I hadn't even published my first book. I simply attended the London Book Fair with a copy of the book's cover design and a list of ten other books I claimed that I would publish in the next year. It was this list of books that

persuaded them to give me a chance. As it turned out, most of those particular book ideas never saw the light of day, but I did carry on publishing other books.

My sales to bookshops across the nation started with taking the back seat out of my car, filling it with books, printing some order forms, delivery notes and information sheets, and heading off on a national bookshop tour. I would nip in, without an appointment, grab the attention of someone on the shop floor, show them my book and describe it in less than thirty seconds. If they wanted to stock it I would write their details on the order form and give them the books immediately from my bag or fetch them from the car. This saved a fortune in delivery costs. An invoice would be issued when I got home.

How do I design the paperwork for taking orders?

The various items of stationery you need to sell your book are listed below together with the information fields each should contain. You can download simple templates for each form from my website: www.stewartferris.com.

Advance Information sheet

This is known in the book trade as an AI sheet. It's an A4 sheet of paper, printed on one side only, containing all the information a bookseller needs to be able to make a purchasing decision:

- The book cover in colour (no larger than a quarter of the page size)

- The title, subtitle and author name

- The price, ISBN, binding, page count, dimensions, and publication date

- The blurb

- Information about the author

- Key selling points

- The publisher's name, logo and contact details

Order form

This should be either A4 or A5 in size, printed on one side only, containing your publisher contact details, the title of the book, the ISBN and the price. Next to that should be a box in which the shop manager can write their desired order quantity. Somewhere on the page should also be boxes in which the shop's name and address can be written, plus the date and an order reference. Many shops won't let you take the order form away with you there and then: they'll insist on hanging onto it until they're ready to order it themselves.

Delivery note

This is almost identical to the order form, except that it also has a line simply stating 'Received by [NAME] and [SIGNATURE]'.

Mail Order

Your mail order sales are most likely to come from a website, if you set one up, or from local and national printed features and advertising. Every copy of your book sold by mail order makes a larger profit margin than one sold through a bookshop because you don't have to give away any discount. You can even make a little profit on the postage and packaging charge. The level of mail order sales you achieve will depend entirely on the extent and type of exposure you create for your book.

Amazon

The moment you register your book's details with the ISBN agency that information will appear on the Amazon website. If someone attempts to buy the book from Amazon the order will be passed either to one of the big wholesalers or directly to you, using the information you supplied to the ISBN agency. The dispatch time stated for your book on the website can be reduced to just one day if you join the Amazon Advantage scheme. Under this system, a few copies of your book will be held by Amazon on consignment so that they can deliver it to the customer more quickly, and they will pay you monthly for any copies sold. Full information about the Amazon Advantage scheme can be found at www.amazon.co.uk/advantage.

Make the most of your book's Amazon page by uploading as much information about yourself and your book as you can using the link available at the bottom of the page. You can place a sample of your text, a table of contents, your own comments about the book and much more. Experience has shown that books with more information on Amazon outperform those with only minimal data.

Other Internet sales

The domination of Amazon in the Internet book market is almost 100 per cent. Plenty of other Internet bookshops exist, but they attract so little sales that it probably isn't worth spending too much time worrying about them. But it is worth tracking down specialist websites that are relevant to your book and trying to persuade the site owners to feature your book – if they do so, chances are the customer will be redirected to Amazon in order to complete the purchase.

Signed copies sold on eBay

Many people thin out their book collections by selling old books on eBay. Signed copies attract a premium price, and you have a distinct advantage here: you can autograph every copy you sell. If you run one auction a week on eBay, assuming you're able to attract sufficiently high bids to make it profitable (if you can sell for as little as half the retail price of the book it's the equivalent of selling a copy through a bookshop), it will increase your annual sales by 50 copies.

Let's take a hypothetical example of how many books might be sold in one year using the methods and paperwork listed above.

Friends and family	20
Social networking sites	5
Organisations	70
Local shops	200
National shops	500
Mail order	50
Amazon	100
Other Internet sales	5
Signed copies sold on eBay	50

That comes to a total of 1,000 books sold in a year by exploiting all the possible sales avenues. Of course, some are more important than others, but you need all of them to shift an entire print run within a reasonable time frame.

How can I take enough orders to pre-sell all the copies before the books are even printed?

1. Secure an order from a major high street bookshop chain. This is easier said than done, and if all publishers were able to pre-sell entire prints like this every time they published a book there would be Rolls Royces in publishers' car parks instead of Volvos. Many of the big name high street stores won't even see you at their head office. But policies change and there's no harm in trying to get an appointment. If you can't get to see the buyers for these companies then send them an Advance Information sheet detailing everything they need to know about the book. Also send them samples of the typeset pages, publicity information and reasons why this book needs to be stocked nationally. Getting a head office order like this for thousands of copies is a bit of a long shot, but it has happened before and it's certainly more likely than winning the lottery.

2. Get in your car and go and visit dozens of bookshops, taking small orders from each one. This is the way most publishers have worked

for many years, sending representatives all over the country to obtain small orders from individual shops until they have enough orders in total to justify a print run. It's not easy, though, and you'd better be good at handling rejection. I've had occasions when I'd driven for half a day to visit one particular shop only to be told they don't want to order any books from me. It's all part of the job.

3. Place a subscription list in the back of the book. People like to see their name in print, and I once used this fact to pre-sell a local history book. Anyone who ordered their copy at least a couple of months before the publication date had their name listed at the back of the book. With some free publicity in the local newspaper, a website and plenty of leaflets, I was able to raise enough cash from advance sales to pay for the print run before the book was even typeset. This technique lends itself particularly well to local interest books, but could function equally well for books of interest to particular associations, charities or societies through their newsletters and websites.

How to outsell the big boys

It's difficult being the underdog. You don't have the advertising budget, the glossy promotional materials and the teams of people from which a large publisher benefits. But your book has to hold its own out there in the bookshops. It's competing for shelf space with books from multinational companies. Without knowing it, you have one secret weapon that they don't have; one huge advantage over them. The advantage is this: large publishers are producing new books at a rate of one a week, or even one a day. If it's one a week then the staff who are involved in selling that book can only focus on it for one week before moving onto the next book. It's not quite so clear cut as this in reality, but the principle is sound.

Even if they have a team of four salespeople to push the book, each of them can only give it their undivided attention for a week. Five days per person, in fact. Twenty days in total. Then that's it. They're pushing the next book, and then the next one. Very rarely do they have time to go back and promote their backlist. Even if they had the time, the bookshops wouldn't want to know. If a shop has made the decision to stock the book they don't want the publisher hassling them about it. The publisher lets them get on with it. When it's time to visit that shop again, the publisher is concerned with selling in the next new book, not the old one. Whereas you, as a self-publisher with only one book to sell for, perhaps, the next year or even longer, can do things differently. You can be a thorn in the bookseller's side, constantly checking the quantity of stock and its position in the shop, constantly requesting reorders when the stock sells through.

I've seen self-published authors obtain bulk orders for their books from high street chains simply by being annoying. They write letters, send e-mails and regularly phone the head office buyers until finally these buyers give in, order the books, and pray that the daily assault on their in-boxes will cease. I'm not recommending this as a business practice, because senior book buyers are important people and need to be allowed the space to do their jobs, but it shows what a determined and focused author can achieve. On a smaller scale, the same thing can be achieved with local bookshop branches.

By staying on top of things, never losing sight of the performance of your book in any shop in your local area, you can sustain steady sales throughout the year when a mainstream publisher would probably experience declining sales because they don't have the resources to monitor things so closely.

What other ways can I make money from my book, aside from selling copies of it?

THE FOLLOWING LIST covers ways that it is theoretically possible to make money from your book other than actually selling the printed copies. All of the sources of income are referred to as 'subsidiary rights'. The right to use your written words in any way other than your own printed edition is something for which people might pay money. The actual chances of making a sale of any of these rights are pretty slim: established publishers, on average, only manage to sell one or two rights from the list for each book they publish. For the beginner it's a much more difficult task because it takes years to develop contacts in the industry and a reputation for creating commercially viable products. But it's important to be aware of the potential that exists and you should make your own judgement as to whether to pursue these kinds of sales.

Translation rights
This is the right to publish your book in a foreign language. When a publisher buys the right from you to publish in their language, they take responsibility for organising their own translation. All you do is

sign the contract, accept the advance on royalties, and, if the foreign edition is successful, wait for annual royalty payments. Essentially, you become an author with a foreign publisher, that's all.

It's possible to sell translation rights by mailing copies of your book to potential overseas publishers, but finding out who are the best potential publishers for your book in dozens of countries is difficult. Attendance at international book fairs is the only reliable way of meeting potential publishers and seeing at a glance whether your book would fit their list. The world's largest book fair is the Frankfurt Book Fair, held every October. In three or four days you have the opportunity to present your book to about ten thousand publishers from around the world. There is also the London Book Fair, held in the spring, although it is only a tenth of the size of its German equivalent so there will be fewer publishers to meet.

English language rights overseas

This is the right to publish another English edition in a different English-speaking country. Some spellings, measurements and currencies may be localised (localized for the US edition!). An advance on royalties is normally paid, followed by annual royalty payments if the book is a hit.

Large print rights

Some publishers specialise in large print editions of popular books for elderly and partially sighted readers. They pay an advance on royalties for the large print rights and, although the book will be sold in the same country as your own edition, it won't compete with yours as most large print sales are to libraries rather than to bookshops.

Extract or serial rights

Newspapers and magazines pay for the right to use a chunk of your text as an article or a series of articles. Not only do you get paid for this, but you also get excellent sales-boosting publicity for your book.

Film options

The option to make a movie from your story. It is possible to make money from such rights over and over again without any film ever being made. Producers pay for the 'option' to make the film, and that option has a time limit. Commonly it is between six and eighteen months, although it can last longer. The producer won't pay huge sums of cash for the option, but if at the end of the time period specified in the contract they haven't bought the full rights to make the film then the option expires and you're free to sell it to someone else. The reason they buy options is that it gives them time to try to raise finance to make the film, safe in the knowledge that you won't sell the film rights to someone else during the period of the contract. The same applies to television options.

Film rights

The right to make a movie from your story. This is the full monty, and the sums paid for film rights are huge compared to the amounts paid for options. But it still doesn't guarantee a film will get made: Hollywood movie companies have been known to buy film rights to a book that they have no intention of adapting, merely to prevent the competition from creating a movie from the same book.

Audio rights

The right to make and sell a sound recording of your book. Cassette and CD products are still being made for this market, but the future will be in audio files that can be downloaded from the Internet. An advance on royalties would normally be paid for these rights.

What is online publishing?

ONLINE PUBLISHING MEANS making your book available on the Internet for sale (or for free) as a downloadable electronic file. It's possible to do this simply by uploading your Word file, but it looks more professional to turn your manuscript into something which more closely resembles the pages of a book. A book sold in downloadable form on the Internet is called an eBook.

Customers can read eBooks on their desktop or laptop computers, on their mobile phones and on other portable electronic devices and specialist eBook readers. The market for eBooks is small but growing steadily and it's worth making the effort to publish your book in an electronic format so that it can remain 'in print' forever, whether or not any physical stock exists.

Types of eBook

The most common formats of eBooks are PDF, Mobipocket, Palm and Microsoft Reader. The viewing software for all of these formats is free for anyone to download.

How do I create the various types of eBook?

The software needed to produce eBook files takes some getting used to and involves working with text files, html files and various kinds of image files. If you want to have a go, you can try the following packages:

Type of eBook	Software needed to create it
PDF	Adobe Acrobat
Mobipocket	Mobipocket Creator
Palm	Palm DropBook
Microsoft Reader	ReaderWorks Publisher

Some websites will do the eBook creation for you: all you need to do is upload the Word document and create a cover design using their own templates. This won't create a high quality layout like you've strived to achieve in your printed edition, but at least it will get your words on sale in electronic form. Visit www.ebookmall.com for more information.

Is it necessary to offer more than one type of eBook?

The more formats you can make your book available in the wider your potential market. The reason why some potential customers might be excluded from buying your eBook if you only offer it, for instance, as a PDF, is that they might want to download to a small portable device rather than to a computer. PDFs create rigid pages which are far too large to view on a mobile phone, so that kind of file will only sell to customers who come across your web page whilst sitting at their computer.

Should the selling price be cheaper than for an equivalent printed book?

Surprisingly, the answer is no. I've published hundreds of eBooks, most of which were eBook editions of existing printed books. At first I sold them online at a cheaper price than the printed versions, then I started to bring the prices in line with each other and was pleased to discover that there was no drop in sales. Customers seem to be prepared to pay full price for an eBook even though the costs of producing and delivering that eBook are far lower for the publisher concerned. So the profit margin on every eBook you sell will be far higher than that of a printed version, but eBook sales in general are currently very small compared to the sales of printed books.

Do I still need an ISBN?

Strictly speaking the eBook edition of your book should have a different ISBN to the printed version, but it's common practice among publishers to use the ISBN of the print edition for the eBook too.

How do I stop people from copying the eBook file?

EBook creation software has options for applying different levels of security to your book. Files can be set in such a way that once downloaded they cannot be copied to another computer, or they can only be copied a set number of times. It's even possible to set eBook files to self-destruct after a predetermined period of time has elapsed.

Other security options include whether to allow the customer to print the file and whether to allow their reader software to use its read-aloud, synthesised voice function.

The important thing to remember is that no security setting can ever protect you completely. A determined copyright infringer may be able to crack the security settings that you apply, but moreover, anyone could simply retype your words into their own word processor file and sell that. If people can see your words they can copy them. The same is true of printed books. In fact, it's really quite easy to copy a printed book with a scanner and character recognition software. So take reasonable precautions, using the options available to you in the software you use to create your eBook, but remember that if anyone does ever pirate your work it's unlikely to be on a large scale. They won't be able to sell the files on any official eBook websites and the occasional small-scale infringement is just something that all publishers have to live with.

Where can I sell my eBook?

There's no need to worry about adding shopping cart and download facilities to your own website in order to sell eBooks. You're unlikely to sell enough downloads to justify the cost. But there are dozens of websites across the world that will sell self-published eBooks, and it won't cost anything to register with them and upload your book. Most of them will take at least half of the money from each sale, and will pay you quarterly. With an eBook on sale it means that even while you're sleeping your book is slowly and steadily bringing in the pennies for you.

A list of websites that sell self-published eBooks is available on my website: www. stewartferris.com.

vays write from the heart.
- Strong central character
- Sub-plot?

THINGS TO CONSIDER
• Finding an agent
• Overcoming writer's block
riter should always
a notebook & pen.

Other writing and publishing guides from Summersdale...

ays write from the heart.
- Strong central character
- Sub-plot?

THINGS TO CONSIDER
• Finding an agent.
• Overcoming writer's block
...iter should always
...a notebook & pen.

How to be a **Writer**
Secrets from the inside

Stewart Ferris

How to get Published
Stewart Ferris
Strong central character
Sub-plot?
THINGS TO CONSIDER
• Finding an agent.
• Overcoming writer's block.
How to get Published
Secrets from the inside
Stewart Ferris

How to be a Bestselling Novelist
Richard Joseph
- Strong central character
- Sub-plot?
THINGS TO CONSIDER
• Finding an agent
• Overcoming writer's block
How to be a
Bestselling Novelist
Secrets from the inside
Richard Joseph

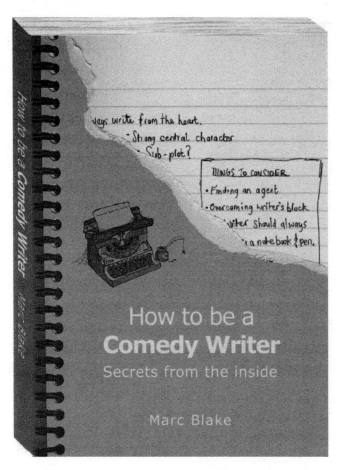

vays write from the heart.
- Strong central character
- Sub-plot?

THINGS TO CONSIDER
• Finding an agent
• Overcoming writer's block
  vriter should always
  i a notebook & pen.

How to be a
Comedy Writer
Secrets from the inside

Marc Blake

Study the form.
to avoid.
How long is a script?
• Options and agents.
Catchphrases
Where do I begin?
– CHARACTER –
• Using your life
and dialogue)
How to be a
Sitcom Writer
Secrets from the inside
Marc Blake
How to be a Sitcom Writer
Marc Blake

Praise for *How to be a Writer* by Stewart Ferris

'As both a writer and publisher, Stewart Ferris is well qualified to write a book on how to be a writer. Ideal for writers who are just setting out but who have little idea how to go about it'
WRITING MAGAZINE

*'[*How to be a Writer *is a] neat insider's guide to getting started'*
BBC KENT

Praise for *How to be a Sitcom Writer* by Marc Blake

*'*How to be a Sitcom Writer *is amazing value for money. It is packed with practical exercises, guaranteed to improve your sitcom. The author makes you work at developing your stories, developing your characters, checking your plots – everything that goes into good sitcom writing. So if you want to be a sitcom writer, or be a better sitcom writer, buy this book and you may just have the last laugh'*
Suite 101 website

Praise for *How to be a Best-selling Novelist* by Richard Joseph

'Joseph interviews eleven authors, and provides bullet-pointed tips from half a dozen more, providing the reader with the essentials on becoming the "next big thing". A quick, easy read, this book is marked out by its accessibility'
R & R Exeter

www.summersdale.com